A

HISTORY

OF

THE

MYRICKS UNITED METHODIST CHURCH

BY

GAIL E. TERRY

for the
Myricks United Methodist Church

Heritage Books, Inc.

Published 1997 by

HERITAGE BOOKS, INC.
1540E Pointer Ridge Place
Bowie, Maryland 20716
1-800-398-7709

ISBN 0-7884-0712-0

A Complete Catalog Listing Hundreds of Titles
On History, Genealogy, and Americana
Available Free Upon Request

TABLE OF CONTENTS

TABLE OF ILLUSTRATIONS

PREFACE

My grandmother, Mrs. Marian H. Stetson, was a member of the Myricks Methodist Church for 78 years. She served as Church Historian for many years. Shortly before she died, I became interested in her lifelong pursuit of learning about and preserving the past. When I came across her records of the Church I thought they were very interesting. They brought back memories of my childhood and added information about the history of the Church that I did not know. It also brought to life some of the people who lived in Myricks over the past 150 years. I began making notes of the items I found most interesting. My mother, Mrs. Althea L. Stetson, then began bringing home the Church records for me to read, and she indicated there was no written history of the Church. I decided there were probably a lot of local residents who would enjoy knowing more about their church and community, and for these reasons I decided to write this book.

Gail E. Terry

THE MYRICKS METHODIST EPISCOPAL CHURCH
ABOUT 1910

THE MYRICKS UNITED METHODIST CHURCH
1995

Chapter 1

MYRICKS METHODIST CHURCH

Myricks today is a section of the town of Berkley, Massachusetts. Myricks was originally a part of Taunton, Massachusetts, located in the southeastern portion of that city, until April 1879. At that time, Myricks became a part of Berkley at the request of the citizens of Myricks who felt their farming lifestyle was more in tune with the lifestyle of the citizens of Berkley. Church records indicate this area was originally called Myrickville or Myricksville with the last entry by this name in church records on July 29, 1888. Beginning August 5, 1888, entries are made as Myricks.

The first meeting house in the Myrickville section of Taunton was located on County Road near the Fall River and Middleboro Rail Road tracks. Two maps show it was located about where 49 or 51 County Street would be today. It was called the Hoop - pole Meeting House as barrel hoops were made there on the first floor. Religious meetings were held in the single large room on the second floor.

Although there is no proof, the following passage possibly refers to the Hoop - pole Church.

"The Protestant, or Reformed Methodist Church. South Taunton. This branch of the Methodist Church was organized in 1830, consisting of fifteen members. Their meeting-house is several miles from "the Green," and was built in 1832. They

1

have had a succession of ministers, whose names, in part, are as follows: Moses Swift, Ebenezer Spindle, Pliny Britt, Joseph Eldredge, _____ Wheaton, John Eliot."[1]

The following document is the earliest one found regarding the church in Myricks.

"KNOW ALL MEN BY THESE PRESENTS THAT WE, SETH STAPLES and MOSES G. ANDREWS of Taunton, and MILTON PAUL of Berkley, all in the County of Bristol, a Committee duly and legally appointed by vote of a Religious Society which was organized on the fourth day of March one thousand eight hundred and thirty-four, at the Reformed Methodist Meeting-house situated in the easterly part of the said Town of Taunton, to make, execute and deliver deeds of Pews in the above mentioned Meeting-house, to the purchasers thereof, -- in consideration of the sum of Six Dollars to us paid by George S. Hoard of Middleborough in the County of Plymouth for labor done and materials used on said House, situated in Taunton as above, the receipt whereof we do hereby acknowledge, do hereby, in pursuance of the vote aforesaid, grant, sell, convey and confirm to the said George S. Hoard his heirs and assigns, PEW numbered three in the Meeting-house aforesaid, with all the privileges and appurtenances thereto belonging.
TO HAVE and to HOLD the same to the said George S his heirs and assigns forever." [2]

A new house of worship was built in 1853, at 93 Myricks Street, at the corner of Myricks Street (Rhode Island Road) and Church Street (Blind Road). It was built on land owned by the Mirick family. The following article tells about the dedication of the new church on July 14, 1853.

"Dedication at Miricksville. - The Methodist Protestant Church, at Miricksville, erected this season, was dedicated last Thursday. Sermon by Rev. Mr. Lowell, of Boston. The singing was under the direction of Mr. Lorenzo D. Davis, of this city, and was very fine. Revs. Messrs. Upham, of the Pleasant Street, and McKeown, of the Allen Street Church, participated in the services of the occasion. The attendance from this city was quite limited although the house was crowded by the residents of the vicinity. The house has been mainly erected through the efforts of the pastor of the Society, Rev. Moses Brown, for whom a subscription was taken up, at the church, which was quite successful."[3]

The founders of the church appear in the following document which states:

"Know all men by these Presents, That The Methodist Protestant Society in Taunton County of Bristol and State of Massachusetts a Religious Corporation duly organized and established at Myrickville in said Taunton by George S. Hoard, Elbridge G. Staples and John Allen of Taunton in said County, and of Lakeville in the County of Plymouth agents and standing Committee of said Corporation for this purpose duly authorized by a vote passed at a legal meetting of said Society held July 30th 1853..."[4]

An interesting fact is that the "lot" on

which the church was built was not
purchased until January 19, 1854, after
the building was completed.

The Hoop-pole building was sold to Cyrus
O. Elmes after it was no longer being used
as a church, and it was moved to Mill
Street Extension. This building is still
standing today and is used as a residence.

The Mirickville Methodist Protestant
Society was reorganized on April 26, 1871,
as the First Methodist Episcopal Church
Myricksville by Bro. Samuel C. Brown,
Presiding Elder of the Fall River
District. In 1939, three major churches
were united and it became the Myricks
Methodist Church. The Myricks Methodist
Church was incorporated in 1950. In 1968,
it became a United Methodist Church. This
resulted from a marriage between the
Evangelical United Brethren Church and
Methodist Church. On January 26, 1969,
the name of the church officially became
the Myricks United Methodist Church.

A 100th Anniversary celebration and
spiritual housewarming for the hall was
held August 15 and 16, 1953. The
celebration consisted of a two day lawn
party and "old home day". The church
building was dedicated on August 16, 1953.
Dr. Charles M. McConnell was a speaker at
the morning service. After the service a
pot luck dinner was held in the church
hall. Another program was held during the
day with Reverend J. Kenneth Pearson
speaking. The guest book for that day was
signed by 121 people.

By license from the Judge of Probate for the County of Bristol I will be sold at Public auction on Thursday the 19th day of January next at half past one o'clock P. M. the lot on which the Methodist Protestant Church stands, said lot is situated at the four corners near Myricks Depot

Taunton Dec 19th 1853
Sarah C. Myrick Guardian

The above lot was sold January 19th 1854 to the Methodist Protestant society at Myricks &c

Moses Brown
Auctioneer

1854 Document Courtesy of
Merle J. E. Stetson

MYRICKS METHODIST CHURCH BEFORE 1894

1 Emery, Samuel Hopkins <u>The Ministry of Taunton</u> Vol. 2 (Boston: John Jewett and Company 1853) p. 148 - 149.
2 Old Colony Historical Society, Taunton, Massachusetts, Folder VM989C.
3 <u>The Republican Standard,</u> New Bedford, Massachusetts, July 21, 1853, p. 1.
4 Old Colony Historical Society, Taunton, Massachusetts, Folder VM989C.

Chapter 2

DEEDS

The earliest deed after the new church building was erected states that on July 30, 1853, for the sum of $25, Joshua T. Sekell purchased Pew numbered 3. A copy of this deed is located at the Old Colony Historical Society.

Bristol County North District Land Deeds
BOOK 217 Page 171 + 172
"Know all men by these presents that I, Sarah C. Mirick, Guardian of Erastus O. Mirick, Artemas B. Mirick, Sarah J. Mirick and Emily Mirick, all of Taunton, in the County of Bristol, minors, being duly licensed, by the Court of Probate, at a term thereof holden at Seekonk, within and for the County of Bristol, on the Sixth day of September 1853, in pursuance of a Sale at public vendue, held on the nineteenth day of January 1854, and in consideration of Twenty five Dollars paid by the Mirickville Methodist Protestant Society, a Corporation duly established in said Taunton, who was the highest bidder, at the said sale, for the estate herein after described, the receipt whereof I do hereby acknowledge, do hereby grant, bargain, sell, and convey unto the said Mirickville Methodist Protestant Society and their assigns, as and for a Meeting House Lot + for no other purpose, a lot of land situated in Taunton aforesaid, containing forty rods, more or less. Bounded - Beginning at the corner of the Rhode Island and New Bedford roads - thence S. 4° W. in the line of said New Bedford road, twelve rods and two feet,

thence N. 32 1/2 W. eleven and a quarter rods to said Rhode Island road - thence Easterly in the line of said Rhode Island Road, seven rods + two feet to the corner first mentioned - being the same lot upon which said Society has recently erected a Meeting House.

To have and to Hold the same to the said Mirickville Methodist Protestant Society + their assigns, to their use and behoof forever. And I do hereby covenant with the said Society + their assigns, that I am duly empowered to convey the same premises to the said Society, and that I have in all things observed the rules and directions of the law in said sale.

In witness whereof, I have here unto set my hand and seal the Seventeenth day of Februrary eighteen hundred and fifty four. Signed, Sealed and delivered

Sarah C. Mirick

in presence of
Geo. M. Woodward

Bristol ss. February 17, 1854.
Sarah C. Mirick acknowledged the foregoing instrument by her signed to be her free act and deed."

Bristol County North District Land Records
BOOK 217   Page 172
"Before me, Geo. M. Woodward Justice of the Peace
Rec'd July 28, 1854. + recorded by - Joseph Wilbar Register
Know all men by these presents, That I, Sarah C. Mirick of Taunton, in the County of Bristol, in consideration of Twenty five Dollars, paid by the Mirickville Methodist Protestant Society, a Corporation duly established in said Taunton, the receipt whereof is hereby acknowl-

edged, do hereby remise, release, and forever quitclaim, unto the said Mirickville Methodist Protestant Society + their assigns, as and for a Meeting House Lot + for no other purpose, - a lot of land situated in Taunton aforesaid, containing forty rods, more or less. Bounded as follows - Beginning at the corner of the Rhode Island + New Bedford roads - thence South 4° West, in the line of said New Bedford Road, twelve rods and two feet, thence North 32 $1/2^\circ$ West, eleven and a quarter rods, to said Rhode Island road, thence easterly in the line of said Rhode Island road, seven rods and two feet, to the corner first mentioned, being the same lot upon which said Society has recently erected a Meeting House.

To Have and to Hold the above released premises, with all the privilages and appurtenances to the same belonging, to the said Mirickville Methodist Protestant Society + their assigns, to their use and behoof forever.

In witness whereof, I the said Sarah C. Mirick, have hereunto set my hand and Seal this the twenty seventh day of February, in the year of our Lord one thousand eight hundred and fifty four.

Signed, Sealed and delivered

                              Sarah C. Mirick

in presence of
William Haskins

        Bristol ss. February 28th 1854.

Then personally appeared the above named Sarah C. Mirick, and acknowledged the above instrument to be her free act and deed.

Before me, William Haskins Justice of the Peace.

Rec'd July 28, 1854. + recorded by Joseph

11

"Know All men by these Presents, That
Moses Brown of Taunton County of Bristol,
State of Massachusetts, In consideration
of the sum of seventy two dollars and
fifty cts to said Brown paid by Ethern
pierce, and Enus Pierce of Taunton and
Lakeville before the delivery of this
deed, the receipt whereof is hereby
acknowledged, have, and by these presents
do give, grant, sell and convey unto the
said Ethern Pierce and Enus Peirce the Pew
numbered 26 on the floor of the Methodist
Protestant Meeting house erected by said
Society, and situated at Myricksville, in
said Taunton together with all the
privileges and appurtenences to the same
Pew belonging. To have and to Hold the
Pew aforesaid, with the privileges and
appurtenences thereof unto the said Ethern
and Enus Pierce there heirs and assigns,
unto the sole use and behoof of the said
Ethern and Enus Pierce there heirs and
assigns forever, excepting as follows.
First, the Pulpit in said Meeting House
shall be supplied with such Ministers as
the members of the Methodist Protestant
Church worshiping therein shall elect,
from time to time so long as they maintain
their present faith and order. Second:-
this deed shall entitle noone to any
privileges in any private meetings which
are designed for the benefit of the
members of said church exclusively.
Third: no person holding a pew by virtue
of this deed shall have the right or
privilege of altering said pew, unless
authorized by said corporation - or of
injuring, disfiguring or distroying the
same. Fourth: all alterations in the pews

12

of said House, shall be subject to the exclusive controle of said corporation at legal meetings called for that purpose. Fifth: the pew or pews held by virtue of this deed, shall be used exclusively for religious and kindred purposes. Sixth: the expenses of all repairs in, upon, or about said house and lot including painting, purchasing anew the fixtures or furniture, and of insurance against fire, shall be subject to a tax assessed upon, and paid by the owners of pews, according to the valuation thereof before the sale. Seventh: said Meeting House shall at all times be under the immediate care of the trustees or standing committee of the corporation for the time being by whose direction the same shall be opened and closed at all meetings of public or private worship. Meetings of buisiness of the Church corporation, benevolent Societies thereto belonging, and meeting for improvement in sacred music. And the said Brown does hereby covenent with the said Ethern and Enus Pierce there heirs and assigns, that untill the delivery hereof, they are the lawful owners of said Pew, and have good right and lawful authority to sell and dispense of the same. In testimony of the said Brown has caused his name and seal to be hereunto affixed.

The 10th day of February A. D. 1855.
Signed Sealed and delivered in Presence of William Haskins   By Moses Brown Bristol SS. February 10th A. D. 1855 then personally appeared the above named Brown and acknowledged the foregoing instrument by him subscribed, to be his free act and deed.

Before me William Haskins Justice of the

13

Know All Men by these Presents, That Moses Brown of Taunton County of Bristol
State of Massachusetts, In consideration of the sum of seventy two dollars and fifty cts
to said Brown paid by Ethan Pierce and Enus Pierce of Taunton and Seekonville before
the delivery of this deed, the receipt whereof is hereby acknowledged, have, and by
these presents do give grant, sell and convey unto the said Ethan Pierce and
Enus Pierce the Pew Numbered 26 on the floor of the Methodist Protestant meeting house
erected by said society, and situated at Myrecksville, in said Taunton together with
all the privileges and appurtenances to the same Pew belonging. To have and to
Hold the Pew aforesaid, with the privileges and appurtenances thereof unto the
said Ethan and Enus Pierce their heirs and assigns, unto the sole use and behoof
of the said Ethan and Enus Pierce their heirs and assigns forever, excepting as follows
First the Pulpit in said meeting House shall be supplied with such Ministers as the members
of the Methodist Protestant church worshiping therein shall elect, from time to time so long
as they maintain their present faith and order. Second this deed shall entitle no one
to any privileges in any private meetings which are designed for the benefit of the
members of said church exclusively. Third no person holding a pew by virtue of this
deed, shall have the right or privilege of altering said pew, unless authorized by said
corporation or of injuring, disfiguring or destroying the same. Fourth all alterations
in the pews of said House, shall be subject to the exclusive control of said corporation, at
legal meetings called for that purpose. Fifth the pew or pews held by virtue of this
deed, shall be used exclusively for religious and kindred purposes. Sixth the
expenses of all repairs in, upon, or about said house and lot including painting, purchasing and the
fixtures or furniture, and of insurance against fire, shall be subject to a tax assessed upon,
and paid by the owners of pews, according to the valuation thereof before the sale. Seventh
said meeting house shall at all times be under the immediate care of the trustees or standing committee of the corporation
for the time being, by whose direction the same shall be opened and closed at all meetings of public or private worship,
the transacting of business of the church, corporation, or such other uses thereto belonging, and meetings for improvement in sacred science. And
the said Brown does hereby covenant with the said Ethan and Enus Pierce their heirs and assigns, that until the delivery
hereof, they are the lawful owners of said Pews, and have good right and lawful authority to sell and dispose of the same.
In testimony whereof the said Brown has caused his name and seal to be hereunto affixed,
This 10th day of February A. D. 1855.
Signed sealed and delivered in the presence of ___ William Hoskins

By Moses Brown

Bristol S.S. February 10th A. D. 1855 then personally appeared the above
named Brown and acknowledged the foregoing instrument by him subscribed, to be his free act and deed,
Before me William Hoskins

Justice of the Peace

Document from Church Records

Peace"   (Deed from Church Records)

Also, on February 10, 1855, Pew numbered 32 was purchased by George S. Hoard of Lakeville for $73.50, and Pew numbered 6 was purchased by Joshua Padelford for $69.75. These deeds are located at the Old Colony Historical Society, Taunton, Massachusetts, folder VM989C, as are the following two deeds:

"Know all men by these presents that I Moses Brown, of South Braintree in the County of Norfolk in the Commonwealth of Mass. Clergyman, in consideration of three hundred dollars to me paid by the Methodist Protestant Society in Taunton, County of Bristol and Commonwealth afore-said, a Religious Corporation, duly organized and established at Myricksville in said Taunton, and by the Methodist Protestant Church, there organized and worshipping before the delivery of this deed, the receipt whereof, is hereby acknowledged, have and by these Presents do give, grant, sell and convey unto the said Methodist Protestant Society and the said Methodist Protestant Church, and their successors, the Pews One, Fourteen, Fifteen, Sixteen + Twenty Three..." dated April 11, 1856.

"Know All Men by these Presents That I Kesiah H. Myrick of Taunton and County of Bristol Wm C Myrick of Sharon County of Norfolk and Ellen R Anderson in her own right of Jamaica Plain County of Norfolk and Commonwealth of Massachusetts - In consideration of one Dollar paid by the Methodist Episcopal Society in Taunton at Myrickville and Commonwealth aforesaid Do

15

hereby grant sell and convey to the said Society One Pew NO Four in the meeting house of said Society aforesaid -- Warranted free from incumberance and against any adverse claim.

Witness our hands and Seals the 24th day of July 1874.

Executed and delivered in presence of
Tho P. Paull

Georgie M. Willis

Keziah H. Myrick
Wm C Myrick
Ellen R Anderson"

Bristol County Registry of Deeds BOOK 517 Page 422

"Know all Men by these Presents that we Erastus O. Myrick and Eugene C. Myrick both of Providence in the State of Rhode Island and Emily Farmer of Berkley in the Commonwealth of Massachusetts, in consideration of One Dollar paid by William Pierce, Elbridge G. Staples, Otis M. Farmer and Orin H. Atwood as Trustees of the Myricks Methodist Episcopal Church in said Berkley the receipt whereof is hereby acknowledged, do hereby give, grant, bargain, sell and convey unto the said trustees an acre of land in said Berkley adjoining the lot upon which the meeting house of said Society stands, bounded as follows, viz beginning at the northwest corner of said meeting house lot, on the road leading from said meeting house to Myricks station thence by said road westerly one hundred sixty nine and one half (169.50) feet to a corner; thence by land grantors S. 3° W. two hundred (200) feet to a corner; thence easterly parallel to said road two hundred eighty seven (287) feet to the southerly corner of said meeting house lot thence north westerly

16

by said meeting house lot to the point of beginning. Said grantees to build and maintain a good and suitable fence upon the lines adjoining our remaining land so long as we own adjoining. Said lot is part of the land joining our remaining land formerly owned by Calvin Myrick. To Have And To Hold the granted premises, with all the privileges and appurtenances thereto belonging to the said trustees and their successors and assigns, to their own use and behoof forever. And We hereby for ourselves and our heirs, executors and administrators, Covenant with the grantees and their successors and assigns that We - lawfully seized in fee simple of the granted premises, that they are free from all incumbances, that we have good right to sell and convey the same as aforesaid; and that We will and our heirs, executors, and administrators shall Warrant And Defend the same to the grantees and their successors and assigns forever against the lawful claims and demands of all persons. And for the consideration aforesaid we Ednah Myrick wife of said Erastus O. Myrick and Charles W. Farmer husband of said Emily Farmer hereby release unto the grantee - and their successors and assigns all right of or to both Dower and Homestead and an estate by the Curtesy in the granted premises.

In Witness Whereof We the said Erastus O. Myrick, Ednah Myrick, Eugene C. Myrick, Emily Farmer and Charles W. Farmer hereunto set our hands and seals this second day of June in the year one thousand eight hundred and ninety two.
Signed, sealed and delivered

                    Erastus O. Myrick
                    Ednah Myrick

17

Eugene C. Myrick
Emily Farmer
Charles W. Farmer
in presence of Edmund C. Pierce
as to E.O.M., E.M. and E.C.M.
George A. King to E.F. + C.W.F.
State of Rhode Island + c. Providence sc.
In Providence this 14th day of June 1892
Erastus O. Myrick, Ednah Myrick and Eugene
C. Myrick above named personally appeared
and acknowledged the foregoing instrument
to be their free act and deed before me,
Edwin C. Pierce Notary Public.
Commonwealth of Massachusetts.
Bristol ss. Taunton June 2, 1892. Then
personally appeared the above named Emily
Farmer and acknowledged the foregoing
instrument to be her free act and deed,
before me, George A. King Justice of the
Peace.
Rec'd June 6, 1894
+ Recorded by J. E. Wilbar Register"

Bristol County Registry of Deeds BOOK 525
Page 447
"Know all Men by these Presents That We,
Erastus O. Myrick of Providence in the
State of Rhode Island and Emily Farmer of
Berkley in the Commonwealth of Massachu-
setts, In consideration of one hundred
dollars and other valuable considerations
paid by Wm. H. Pierce, Otis M. Farmer,
John F. Allen, Orin H. Atwood and Charlie
G. Staples as Trustees of the Myricks
Methodist Episcopal Church of said
Berkley, the receipt whereof is hereby
acknowledged, do hereby give, grant,
bargain, sell and convey unto the said
Trustees, a lot of land on the southerly
side of the road leading from Middleboro
to Fall River in said Berkley bounded as

18

follows: beginning in the southerly line of said road at a point one hundred eighty eight feet east from land of Charles W. Farmer and wife; thence by said road easterly sixty (60) feet to a corner by the barway; thence S. 38°50' E. two hundred (200) feet to a corner; thence S. 52°50' W. sixty (60) feet to a corner; thence N. 38°50 W. two hundred (200) feet to point of beginning. Being part of the premises formerly owned by Calvin Myrick and our interest being obtained by inheritance and purchase from the other heirs. This conveyance is made subject to the condition that the grantees shall build and maintain suitable fence upon the lines adjoining our remaining land so long as we own adjoining and this is part of the consideration before named. To Have and to Hold the granted premises, with all the privileges and appurtenances thereto belonging to the said Trustees and their successors and assigns to their own use and behoof forever. And we hereby for ourselves and our heirs, executors and administrators covenant with the grantees and their successors and assigns, that we are lawfully seized in fee simple of the granted premises; that they are free from all incumbrances, except said condition about fencing; that we have good right to sell and convey the same as aforesaid; and that we will and our heirs, executors, and administrators shall Warrant and Defend the same to the grantees and their successors and assigns forever against the lawful claims and demands of all persons. And for the consideration aforesaid we, Edna Myrick wife of said Erastus O. Myrick and Charles W. Farmer husband of said Emily Farmer hereby release unto the

19

grantees and their successors and assigns all right of or to both dower and homestead and an estate by the curtesy in the granted premises.

In Witness Whereof. We the said Erastus O. Myrick, Edna Myrick, Emily Farmer and Charles W. Farmer hereunto set our hands and seals this sixth day of September in the year one thousand eight hundred and ninety five

Signed, sealed and delivered

Erastus O. Myrick
Ednah Myrick
Emily Farmer
Charles W. Farmer

in presence of William H. Harrington

J. P. Peirce

Commonwealth of Massachusetts. Bristol ss. September 6th. 1895.

Their personally appeared the above named Emily Farmer and Charles W. Farmer and acknowledged the foregoing instrument to be their free act and deed, before me. J. P. Peirce. Justice of the Peace.

State of Rhode Island and County of Providence sc.

On this ninth day of September A. D. 1895 personally appeared before me Erastus O. Myrick and Ednah Myrick and acknowledged the above to be their free and voluntary act and deed LS Lewis B. Stillman Notary Public

Rec'd Sept. 23. 1895 + Recorded by J. E. Wilbar Register"

Bristol County Registry of Deeds BOOK 624 Page 81

"Know all Men by these Presents that I, Levi P. Churchill of Berkley in the County of Bristol and Commonwealth of Massachusetts in consideration of one dollar and

20

other valuable consideration paid by the Trustees of the Myricks Methodist Episcopal Church of said Berkley the receipt whereof is hereby acknowledged, do hereby give, grant, bargain, sell and convey unto said Trustees of the Myricks Methodist Episcopal Church a tract of land situated in said Berkley, bounded and described as follows, Beginning at a point in the southerly line of the road from said church to the railroad station and running thence Southerly parallel to the westerly line of said church lot and two rods westerly there from to a corner, thence easterly parallel to the southerly line of said church lot and two rods southerly therefrom to the road leading from "Beechwoods" to said church, thence by last named road northerly about two rods to said church lot, thence by said lot S. 75°30' W. 288.30 feet to a corner thence still by said lot N. 4°15' E. 199 feet to first mentioned road; thence by said road westerly about two rods to the point of beginning. Meaning to convey to said trustees a strip of land two rods in width along the westerly and southerly sides of said church lot. To have and hold the granted premises with all the privileges and appurtenances thereto belonging to the said Trustees of the Myricks Methodist Episcopal Church and their successors and assigns to their now use and behoof forever. And thereby for myself and my heirs executors and administative covenant - with the grantees and their successors and assigns, that I am lawfully seized in fee simple of the granted premises, that they are free from all incumbrances that I have good right to sell and convey the same as aforesaid and that I will and my heirs executors and administators shall warrant and defend the same to the grantees and their successors and assigns forever against the lawful claims and demands of all persons. And for the consideration aforesaid I Alice E. Churchill, wife of the said Levi P. Churchill hereby release unto the grantees and their successors and assigns all right of or to both dower and homestead in the granted premises, and all other rights and interests therein.

In Witness Whereof we the said Levi P. Churchill and Alice E. Churchill hereunto set our hands and seals this tenth day of October in the year one thousand nine hundred and six.

Signed and sealed in presence of
J.P. Peirce   Levi P. Churchill
                                Alice E. Churchill
Commonwealth of Massachusetts.
Bristol ss. October 27th. 1906. Then personally appeared the above named L. P. Churchill and acknowledged the foregoing instrument to be his free act and deed. before me,

    J. P. Pierce Justice of the Peace
Rec'd Nov. 5, 1907 + Recorded by Enos D. Williams, Register"

Chapter 3

CHURCH STRUCTURE AND MAINTENANCE

The Myricks Church has a typical white New England meeting house style of architecture. Even until today the church has maintained its structure basically as it was when it was built. The building measures 30 feet by 40 feet. The granite slabs used for the foundation are said to have been quarried from nearby Lakeville, Massachusetts and cut in Myricks at the stone cutting shop on Grove Street.

The following document gives information concerning the building of the church. Unfortunately, there was no date on the document.

"<u>Gentlemen</u> your committee beg leve to report. They have atteneted to theire duty, in settleing with <u>Mr</u> Brown, the tr^{es} of the Society in South Taunton connected with the M. P. Church in that Place, on examining his accounts, thay find that he renders a sattisfactor account for all the mony payed to him, for the purpose of building A Meeting House at Myrickville, also for the mony payed out for that, and sundree purposis, And in footing up the bills in favour, and against, said society, we find a demand against said society in Notes to the amount of $520.32 cts, given by the trustees of said house to <u>Ford</u>, <u>Allen</u>, <u>Pierce</u>, S. C. <u>Myrick</u> for which the said Brown has rendered a sattisfactory account of availible property to the amount of $480.00 to liquidate the above demand.
The $480.00 laying in parts + particles as

follows $334.00 in Society Pews,
and " " " 25.00 in an order given by
Cushman for Blinds on ford & C6/"
and " " " 30.00 payed for Organ by the
said Brown
and " " " 91.00 that the said Brown is
in debt for the Pews he bin Making
_____
480.00
Also $20.00 for furnishing said house,
$17.00 for other expencis for which the
said Brown rendered a sattisfactory
account.
The above submitted to your disposal,

Abraham Pierce 2d
William Haskins
John Allen
George S Hoard
Ethan Peirce"[1]

Originally, there was a steeple with a
weather vane on top. The weather vane was
replaced by an acorn top in November 1882.
The steeple was hit by lightning, and it
was decided it would be safer and cheaper
to remove it than repair it. It was
removed shortly after 1894, and it has
never been replaced.

Mr. Isaac Horton and Mr. Silas Braley,
with the help of Mr. Braley's yoke of
oxen, put the belfry into place. It holds
two bells. The large bell was purchased
in November 1874. The bell weighs 400
pounds. Charles Paull and Mr. J. B.
Washburn were on the committee to purchase
this bell. It was put into place in
December 1875. It was used to summons
parishioners to church by being rung a
quarter hour before the beginning of
services. This bell was also used as a

fire alarm in the early days. Expenses for the bell list $149.50 from the bank, $111.50 from Subscription, and $13.67 from the Sewing Circle for a total of $274.67. The small bell was tolled five minutes before church services began. This small bell was also used when a funeral passed the church. The bell was rung from the time the procession came into sight until it disappeared from view. There is an interesting story about the small bell as told by tradition. In order to purchase the small bell, the members of the church were asked to make donations towards its purchase. One gentleman refused to contribute. It was ironic that his was the first funeral to pass the church after the bell was installed.

Originally, the building had green blinds. The front doors opened into the vestibule which was opposite the door to the Sanctuary. The vestibule went almost all the way across the front of the building. It had a high gallery which was reached by stairs from each end of the vestibule. Here is where the choir loft was found. During the singing of hymns the congregation turned around and faced the choir.

An aisle extended across the back of the Sanctuary and met the two aisles that went down the sides of the church. The center pews were partitioned in the middle, thus four sections of pews were made. The church had seating capacity for 125. The pews were sold to help finance the church. The doors to the pews were numbered and deeds were written when a pew waspurchased (see Chapter 2). A large pulpit, painted black, had stairs leading to it from each side. Four short pews faced the pulpit on both sides.

On each side of the pulpit were tall brass oil lamps. There were four lamp chandeliers in the center of the church. Bracket lamps, perhaps whale oil lamps, were located on the side walls. The Sanctuary was heated by two wood burning stoves that were located in the front corners of the building, and there were long pipes running to the back corners where the chimneys were located.

In 1881 - 82, repairs were made that included removal of the high gallery where the choir sat. The four short pews to the right of the minister were also removed, and a platform was placed there for the choir. The oil lamps were replaced by kerosene lamps. The pew doors were removed to help the air circulate. The numbers were put on the arms of the pews. The pews of regular members had foot stools added so the female members could have their feet off the floor in the cold weather. A new pulpit set, a pulpit, three chairs, two stands, and a communion service ($18) were added. The floor had new carpeting laid, and the church was painted inside and out. A summer entry was also installed. This was all accomplished at a cost of $400.

In 1891, new cushions were purchased for the pews. In 1898, the chimney was repaired. The outside of the church was painted in 1902. The following year repairs were made to the church. It was noted that these repairs were delayed due to sickness and other causes.

The following passage comes from the records of the church:

"12-11-1904 Since our last report our church has passed through much of an unusual character. In <u>Sept.</u> a gale swept through this place so severe that maples and oaks were uprooted and our grove of pines was much damaged. Eight chimneys were blown down through the village, two of this number from the parsonage and one from the church. Damage to the parsonage roof amounted to between 2 + 3 dollars. In October a fire again injured our property but happily no serious loss occurred from this. A Bible Study Class has been formed and is proving <u>helpfull</u>. Thirty hard wood trees have been set out in the church grove as a future protection."

In 1912, the east side of the church was reshingled. On June 7, 1914, it was voted that the doors to the church should swing out instead of in. This work was completed in 1915. In 1916, the church building was valued at $2,500. That same year, it was voted to remove the pews from the south corner and install one stove to help better heat the church.

A new communion set was purchased in April 1920, at a cost of $13.90. In 1920, while a new chimney was under construction, church services were held at the parsonage. A committee comprised of Stephen Dow, Mr. Dean, and Will Copeland began work in 1921, to get electric lights into the village of Myricks and to the church.

In 1922, the outside of the church was painted at a cost of $136.20, plus $27.50 for outside blinds. Samuel Hazzard did this work. He was a whaling seaman who lost his left hand above the wrist in a mill accident. He was able to paint by putting a wire hook over his left forearm to hold the paint pail. He worked alone, including moving ladders. Leon Cudworth painted the inside of the church in November 1922, at a cost of $213. Fireboards for the stoves were also added.

In 1923, a chandelier was placed in the center of the church and side lamps were added. The Christian Church in Assonet gave these as gifts to the Myricks Church. The Ladies' Aid Society placed new carpeting in the sanctuary. An anonymous gift of window shades also improved the interior of the church. In 1923 and 1924, repairs were made at a cost of $819. The altar rail was replaced in 1924. During the pastorate of Reverend M. A. Carter (1925 - 26) electric lights were installed. The work was done through the help of Mr. Alfred Dow and Mr. Stephen A. Dow who had their own electric plant at home and offered to supply the church. In 1927, Taunton agreed to supply Myricks with electricity, and on May 2, 1927, the trustees were authorized to sign a contract for electricity from the City of Taunton. In September 1927, city power was available at the church.

The church purchased a motion picture machine in 1925. To comply with state law there had to be a rear exit. The short pews to the left of the minister were removed, and a door in the rear of the

Sanctuary was added. In 1927, a one pipe heater was installed in the church. This cost $147. In 1928, a side walk was completed. The next year one side of the church was shingled.

In 1934, it was reported that the belfry was in good condition, however it was repaired in 1936. Between 1938 and 1941, the church roof was reshingled and a new ceiling was added. Mr. Clarence C. Trenouth did most of this work. The interior of the church was also painted at this same time and new draperies were hung. The side walk was also repaired, and the windows were puttied.

There are no records found on work completed on the church building between 1941 and 1965. In 1965, the outside of the building was painted. Ernest Stone, Mr. and Mrs. Marshall Walker, Merle Stetson, Walter Craven, Mr. and Mrs. George Travers, Nancy Tibbets, Gregg Travers, Andrea Travers, Bob Morse, and Elwell Perry did this work. Mr. Perry also provided professional assistance and put up new gutters and downspouting. At this time, Albert Comerford resurfaced the church parking lot.

In 1966, new lights were installed in the sanctuary. In 1967, the church was insulated and vinyl siding was applied. In September 1974, Mr. and Mrs. LaVon Linn donated new draperies for the church sanctuary. At this time a shed was removed and the area cleaned up, and new front steps were built.

The doors to the pews were put into

storage in the cabinets in Grove Hall in 1967. In 1967, plumbing work was done and a new leaching bed added. Also, in 1967, a new parking lot was constructed on Myricks Street. Robert Harmon, George Travers, Ronald Erickson, Eric Trites, Charles Ashley and Marshall Walker partially cleared the property on Church Street. On August 8, 1970, a hit and run driver damaged the corner post of the church.

In 1982, a lot of work was accomplished on the church. Two new furnaces were installed. They were purchased with gifts from Mr. and Mrs. LaVon Linn and Cal Overlock. The inside of the church was painted. The roof had been completely reshingled over the previous two years. At the front entrance a new light was installed and railings were added. An outbuilding for tool storage was built. In 1984, the sanctuary was painted. The parking lot was expanded in 1990 - 91.

Janitors of the church have included George Stetson, Percy L. Baldwin and Ronald Adams.

1 Old Colony Historical Society Taunton, Massachusetts, Folder, VM989C.

Chapter 4

GROVE HALL

The building of a hall on church property is noted in the following church record dated September 17, 1892.

"Our people have made a decided improvement to the Church property in clearing their beautiful grove and building a Hall for clam bake ± general purposes. Our Bake was a great success. Mrs. D. Pierce."

On October 25, 1904, a fire in Myricks burned down three houses, a blacksmith shop, and the Myricks school house. On November 7, school reopened at Grove Hall. The school committee had put in windows and desks to accommodate lessons until a new school could be built.

The hall was originally known as the cook house for the clambakes held by the church and as a place to store the dishes and tables. In the Fall of 1905, "Grove Hall" was built as an addition over the original cook house. The work cost $113.02. Grove Hall became a recreation center and place for church suppers. There was a small stage in the hall on which shows were performed for entertainment.

In 1912, it was voted to grant permission to the Myricks Athletic Organization to make alterations to the roof at their cost. In return they were given use of the hall. Grove Hall was painted inside and out in 1923. In June 1924, a 12 foot by 30 foot kitchen was added to the hall.

The hall was wired for electricity in 1925. At a cost of $1.00 each, 100 chairs were purchased. Also in 1925, Grove Hall was given two coats of paint on the outside. Bion Pierce donated the paint, and S. F. Hazzard provided the labor for $45.40.

In the 1920's, a 50th Wedding Anniversary party was held at the Hall for Mr. and Mrs. Charles Wade. Reverend George Brown "remarried" them, with their children Albert E., Howard A., and Mrs. John (Bertha) Perry as attendants. Their granddaughter, Lillian Wade Perry, was also in the party. Approximately 100 guests attended the celebration.

In the late 1920's, a play, "Windy Willows", was put on at Grove Hall. Reverend George Smith Brown, George Stetson, Earland Brailey, Alfred Dow, James Garrity, Dorris P. Brown, Lillian York, and Mrs. Josephine Forrest were the actors in the play.

In 1936, the Womens' Friendly Society paid to have new roofing paper put on the hall. The Church Bulletin on April 12, 1936 listed:

"APR 22 - 8 P. M. Auspires Ladies' Aid, PLAY, "How the Club was Formed" by "The Winners" of Nemasket Grange, Middleboro, at Grove Hall 25 cents."

A hurricane in 1944, ruined the church's grove at Grove Hall.

In 1947, a new Grove Hall building committee was formed. Daniel B. Jones,

Clarence C. Trenouth, George W. Stetson, Robert H. Hunter, Percy L. Baldwin, Ernest Stone, and Reverend Joseph Pritchard were members of this committee. The committee bid on a number of buildings at different times. In September 1947, they applied to the War Assets Administration to purchase Chapel No. 223 in Davisville, Rhode Island. They bid $470 but did not win the bid.

In October, that same year, they asked, Honorable Joseph W. Martin Jr., House of Representatives, about a building, as they had heard seventy-five buildings at Camp Edwards in Falmouth, Massachusetts were to be sold in about three weeks. They successfully bid $615 on a group of six buildings formerly used as prison barracks at the camp. Daniel Jones loaned the church $500 to help pay for the buildings.

The buildings were dismantled and transported to Myricks during the winter of 1947 - 48. Clarence C. Trenouth provided much of the labor and all of the transportation. George Campbell, Richard Billard, and John Atkins provided labor from December 8, 1947 until March 27, 1948. They usually worked eight hours a day, Monday through Friday.

The following is taken from the church records regarding the dismantling of the buildings at Camp Edwards:

"The winter of 1947 and 1948 was a very severe winter, the snow came the last of November and stayed on the ground until late in the spring with more snow added every few days. This delayed the work a

OLD GROVE HALL

MR. and MRS. CHARLES WADE

great deal, every day before starting to work it was necessary to shovel the snow away, it was also necessary to keep a fire going to keep warm as long as there was enough of a building left to keep a stove in."

Paul Trenouth, Richard Babbitt, Daniel Jones, Reverend Pritchard, Wendell Conant, James Garrity, and Everett Frizzell also helped before the building was started. Thomas Brothers, General Contractors, of Middleboro, Massachusetts poured the cement foundation for the new Grove Hall in the fall of 1948. The labor and materials for the foundation cost $950.

In December 1949, the committee applied to the Church Extention Section located in Philadelphia, Pennsylvania for a loan and a donation. A loan was given for $2,000, and a donation of $250 was received. Also, Mr. and Mrs. Clarence C. Trenouth, Mr. and Mrs. George W. Stetson, and Reverend and Mrs. Joseph Pritchard travelled to New York hoping to secure funds from the church board. They received $100.

The new hall's main building measured 30 feet by 60 feet with a 14 foot ceiling. It was attached to the church by a 10 foot by 25 foot extension. It had an attached 30 foot by 15 foot kitchen. There was also a stage which measured 30 feet by 14 feet. All of the labor in building the new hall was donated with the exception of the foundation. The value of the new hall was $22,000 when completed.

Sometime after 1951, when the new Grove

THE
MYRICKS METHODIST CHURCH

JOSEPH H. PRITCHARD, Minister
Telephone: Taunton 1187W3

HOW MUCH DOES THIS CHURCH MEAN TO YOU? . . .

4. The necessary money can be raised by the united effort and consecrated giving of every person in the parish.

THE PLAN FOR FINANCING . . .

The total cost of the building and improvement program outlined in this pamphlet has been estimated at $4,500.00, at least half of which must be raised in our community. The Official Board of the church has adopted the following procedure to raise the money:

1. Let every family or individual decide how much they can give to the project between May 1, 1947 and January 1, 1948. This decision should be made after careful consideration of the importance of the project in relation to the lives of our children and the future of this community. Now is the opportune time. Conditions may never be so favorable again.

2. On Sunday, April 20, visitors will go out from the church to every home in the parish to receive the pledges. A visitor will call in your home between the hours of 2:00 and 4:30 in the afternoon. Be prepared to give him your pledge, and a cash installment, if you desire.

3. Frequent reports will be made by the treasurer of the building fund, and the progress of the campaign will be charted on a thermometer in the church.

COOPERATION IS THE KEYNOTE.

THE SUCCESS OF THIS PROJECT DEPENDS ON ALL OF US— IT DEPENDS ON YOU.

How Much DOES This Church Mean To You ???

37

IT HAS A PROGRAM . . .

WORSHIP:

This church attempts to present a worship service which is orderly and dignified, yet intimate. The service is intended to give expression to the great moods of worship, and thus lead every person into a new sense of harmony with God and man.

RELIGIOUS EDUCATION:

The Sunday School provides religious training for children and young people, realizing nothing in this atomic age should take priority over man's moral and spiritual development.

GROUP PROGRAMS:

These are set up for various ages and interests within the church.

The Woman's Society of Christian Service is the organization through which the women of the church carry out their special interests and activities. The local society meets on alternate Wednesdays at 2:00 for the study sessions and work on projects.

The Myrick's Adult Fellowship invites all adult persons of the parish to membership in this popular group, whose purpose is to support the program of the church, and to promote good fellowship among the adults of the community through social activities. The group meets on the first Wednesday evening of each month at 8:00.

The Myricks Youth Fellowship provides a full program of church-related activities for the young people of the parish. The Youth Choir offers special music for the worship services of the church.

The church sponsors many special services and social activities for the community. Truly, the church is the heart of community life in Myricks.

. . . AND IT HAS OBJECTIVES

To provide a sanctuary which is more conducive to worship than the present "meeting house" type of interior. This can be accomplished by the construction of a chancel where the platform is now, and by the installation of an organ.

To provide better facilities for religious education, group meetings, social events, and other parish activities. At present, four Sunday School classes are conducted in the same room, and there is no place for a much needed adult class to meet. Grove Hall is now wholly inadequate for meetings, suppers, parties, or entertainments. Myricks has no place for young people to gather under favorable conditions.

In order to better serve the community the church proposes to build a combination religious education building and parish hall, to be joined to the present church structure. This building will be designed for use by the Sunday School, and will be adaptable for all the activities which were indicated above. In addition to these, the church will be able to greatly expand its program and increase its services to the community.

HOW IT CAN BE DONE . . .

1. A building can be purchased from the Corps of Army Engineers, to be torn down, and the lumber and other materials to be used in the construction of our building.

2. A gift of $250.00, and a loan of $2,000.00 can be secured from the Board of Missions and Church Extension of the Methodist Church.

3. Much of the work will be done by the men of the parish, thus greatly reducing the cost of skilled labor.

Hall was completed, the old hall was burned down. In the winter of 1953, 200 people were served at one time in the new hall. The usual attendance for church suppers had been 100.

The hall was painted in 1961. In 1974, Mrs. Bion Pierce made and hung curtains in the stage area.

In 1979, Grove Hall was remodeled into a Senior Citizens Center. A $20,000 grant from the federal government to the Council on Aging was given to make the renovations which included fireproofing, wall to wall carpeting, new lighting, new toilets, new storage room, and improved accessibility. The state also provided $1,492 to replace the equipment in the kitchen and to install telephones. The Town of Berkley provided over $2,500. The work on the Council on Aging Senior Center was completed in September 1979. In 1979, there were 268 seniors who participated in sponsored events such as free flu shot clinics, health counseling sessions and blood tests for anemia and sugar diabetes.

Al-A-Teen, AA, Berkley Athletics Association, Cub Scouts, Girl Scouts, and the Berkley Historical Society were other groups meeting at Grove Hall in the 1980's and 1990's.

WORKING ON INSIDE OF NEW GROVE HALL

George W. Stetson, Daniel Jones,
Percy Baldwin, and Clarence C. Trenouth

NEW GROVE HALL

41

Chapter 5

THURBER WING

The Thurber Wing was made possible when $48,000 was received from the Estate of Wesley and Charles Thurber, and a $12,000 gift came from the Thurber Estate. Charles S. Thurber served as pastor of the Myricks church from 1898 - 1901. His son, Wesley E. Thurber, kept in touch with the church after his father was reassigned. Wesley attended church suppers and always left an additional donation after the meal.

Andrea Perry and Marie Nolan were co-chairmen of the building committee for the Thurber Wing. Sandra Kelley, Brian Perry, Stanley Kelley, Richard Carlson, Mike Nolan, and Reverend Susan Carlson were committee members.

Work on the Thurber Wing began on September 23, 1990, when a ground breaking ceremony was held. This was an appropriate date to begin as it was "Christian Education Sunday."

The building measures 28 feet by 46 feet and provides space for educational programs, meetings, a nursery, and a Pastor's Study.

District Superintendent Frances Swartz consecrated the Thurber Wing on April 21, 1991. Carol White, a relative of Charles and Wesley Thurber, attended the ceremony.

A plaque in the wing reads:

THE THURBER WING
IN MEMORY
OF
REVEREND CHARLES S. THURBER
MAY 22, 1864 - AUGUST 10, 1955
PASTOR AT MYRICKS 1898 - 1901
AND
HIS DEDICATED SON
WESLEY E. THURBER
APRIL 30, 1894 - FEBRUARY 24, 1988
MYRICKS UNITED METHODIST CHURCH
BERKLEY, MASSACHUSETTS
APRIL 21, 1991

THURBER WING (Far Right)
1995

45

Chapter 6

PARSONAGE

The first record showing interest in having a parsonage was dated December 10, 1871. In that report, John Seekell, Joshua Padelford and George Hoard were listed as the Parsonage and Furniture Committee. Officers of the Ladies Sewing Circle were later listed as the committee members. In 1883, the pastor was authorized to solicit funds for the building of a parsonage.

Hephzibah Davis Taylor, who lived on the second floor of the house at 168 Padelford Street, left a bequest of $500 and her good Empire furniture to the Myricks Church when she died on September 4, 1894. The church members decided that the money would be best spent on a parsonage that they had been hoping to build. Mrs. Alice Paull and Mrs. Fanny Pierce, among others, were members of the parsonage committee at this time.

The parsonage was built at 75 Myricks Street in 1895, at a cost of $1,400. It had eight rooms. The piazza was added sometime before December 1906, making it a more attractive house. In 1922, the parsonage was painted at a cost of $108.57.

When a fire swept through Myricks on November 15, 1922, the parsonage was severely scorched. Another fire occurred in Myricks on June 1, 1923. The following information was taken from the 4th Quarterly Conference report of

December 26, 1923:

"On Friday June 1st your pastor was expected to attend a meeting in New Bedford at the call of the <u>Dist. Supt.</u> it was well that we did not go for had we been away from home the parsonage might have suffered the same fate as the other buildings did as it was we had a very close call for it caught fire in many places but with the help of others we saved the property with only a damage of about $55.00 which was covered by insurance."

Electric lights were installed in the parsonage in September 1926. In 1926, it was decided the pines surrounding the church were posing a danger, and they were cut down. A double car garage at the parsonage was built with the lumber from these pine trees. Initially, one stall was rented, and one stall was made available to the minister. In 1934, some repairs were made to the parsonage. In 1936, a bathroom was installed. In 1947 - 48, the parsonage was papered and painted with materials and labor being donated by members of the congregation. In 1960, shrubbery was planted at the parsonage. Repairs were made to the cellar and porch in 1968.

The parsonage was sold in 1978, when it was no longer needed, and the upkeep became expensive. Elwell Perry Jr., who purchased the parsonage, placed a plaque on the front of the house marking the residence as the former parsonage.

A note of interest is that Hephzibah

Taylor and her husband Benjamin B. Taylor
are buried at the grave yard on South
Street East in Raynham, Massachusetts.
Their graves are marked by a tall stone
with the following inscriptions:

HEPHZIBAH DAVIS
WIFE OF BENJAMIN B TAYLOR
BORN APRIL 19, 1818.
DIED SEPT. 4, 1894.

BENJAMIN B TAYLOR
BORN AUG. 2, 1808.
DIED JAN. 30, 1875.

BENJAMIN D
SON OF
BENJAMIN B
AND HEPHZIBAH DAVIS
BORN MARCH 18, 1837.
DIED FEB. 25, 1840.

PAUL TAYLOR
DIED APRIL 1, 1848.
AGED 56 YEARS

PARSONAGE BEFORE DECEMBER 1906

Picture Courtesy of
Mr. and Mrs. Arnold Silvan

50

Chapter 7

MEMBERSHIP

The membership of the Myricks Methodist Church has always been rather small.

1871 17	1904 20	1924 28	1975 93
1872 20	1912 14	1935 53	1980 86
1873 29	1914 13	1951 71	1982 43
1894 27	1917 31	1965 99	1984 69

The members of the church in 1871 are listed in one of the earliest church records. It reads:

"The Protestant Methodist Church of Myrickville signified its intention and willingness to unite with the Methodist Episcopal Church April 6th 1871 accordingly the following named united with the First Methodist Episcopal Church Taunton. E G Staples, Amos Wade, Eliza C Wade, Barzillia Staples, Sally Staples, G S Hoard, Sarah C Myrick, Joshua Padelford, Jerusha Padelford, Charity W Staples, Phebe Farmer, Mary A Sekell, Eliza A Padelford, Geo W Reed, Adeline Johnson, Enoch D Staples and Susan Staples.
The following is the certificate of the Pastor.
This certifies that the above named have been acceptable members of the First Methodist Episcopal Church Taunton.

L. B. Bates Pastor"

Several revivals have been held; they helped increase membership in the church. Reverend Gammons held the first one about 1871, after it became a Methodist

Episcopal Church. During the pastoral of J. B. Washburn, 1875 - 77, another revival was held with about twenty professing conversion. In 1916, Reverend Kent held a revival, and in 1985, Reverend Alan Previto held the most recent revival.

Church records indicate that on October 6, 1872, "Eight more united with the Church - namely - William Pierce, his wife Fanny, and daughter Amy, James Dean, and Helen his wife. Sarah J Hoard, and Melvina Haskins, the first a widow the second the wife of a good yet ungodly husband, Melissa Farmer, the wife of Otis Farmer, who was baptized but has not joined the church, the last named two were one year ago, the leaders of the dance."

Ruby Winslow, George W. Stetson, Lillian York, Rita York, Earland Brailey, Daniel Moorehouse, Viola Parris, William Parris, and Gerald Brailey became members in 1926. On March 12, 1926, Mrs. Brailey was voted full membership.

MEMBERSHIP 1931
MEMBERS IN FULL

Lottie E. Adams	Hassabie Migdelny
Ruth R. Ames	Helen C. Paull
Amy Anthony	Edgar C. Reynolds
Elsie L. Bessee	Sarah I. Reynolds
Earland W. Brailey	Annie Sellars
Elsie Bertha Brailey	Ethel G. Sellars
Gerald S. Brailey	Freeman G. Sellars
Lyle Edgar Brailey	Belle Somerskill
Silas Edgar Brailey	Percival F. Staples
E. Josephine Bromley	George W. Stetson
Eleanor Bromley	Marian H. Stetson
Ernest Bromley	Charles F. Washburn
Winifred Bromley	Forrest E. Washburn

Abbie E. Copeland
Ruth C. Day
Frank DeMaranville
E. May DeMaranville
Lillian R. Garrity
Coldie A. Haverstock
Lena F. Henshaw
Bernice L. Holmes
Marietta Horton
Isabella Ingham
Beatrice Jack
Dorothy B. Jack

Gordon L. Washburn
Lena M. Washburn
Edith S. Whitman
Hannah Williams
Grant A. Wilson
Mary J. Wilson
Gilbert W. Winslow
Ruby Z. Winslow
Charles B. Wordell
Grace D. Wordell
Rita A. York

NON-RESIDENT INACTIVE MEMBERS
Harold W. Ashley
Ruth L. Ashley
William Copeland
Anthony P. Dean

William F. Haskins
Marion A. McCarthy
Daniel Moorehouse
Amy F. Paull
Clarence Washburn

PREPARATORY MEMBERS
Ernest H. Brailey
Velma Holmes

On Easter Sunday 1966, Mrs. Lena Henshaw
and Mr. Freeman Sellars were honored as 50
year members. In May 1966, Marian Stetson
was presented with a book on the occasion
of her 50th year of membership. On Easter
Sunday, April 1977, three members received
50 year membership pins. Mrs. LaVon Linn,
George W. Stetson, and Earland Brailey
were the three recognized. Also, Marian
Stetson received a pin for 60 years of
membership. Reverend Richard Dean and
Mrs. Bion Pierce presented the pins.
George and Marian Stetson's daughter, Mrs.
Patricia DeArruda, was organist, and their
grandchildren, Mr. and Mrs. Douglas
Stetson, James DeArruda and June Stetson
sang in a quartet during this service.

MEMBERSHIP 1968

Phyllis Adams	Patricia Perry
Elizabeth Allen	Hillman Poole
Roger Allen	J. B. Richardson
Edith Ames	Zelda Richardson
Frank Ames	Albert Santos
Marie Arnold	Carolyn Sedgley
David Ashley	John Sedgley
Holly Bearse	Freeman G. Sellars
Elsie Besse	Lena Staples
Ethel Bindon	Percival G. Staples
James Bindon	Althea Stetson
Patricia Bowlin	Douglas Stetson
Earland Brailey	Gail Stetson
Ernest Brailey	George Stetson
Harriette Brailey	G. Robert Stetson, Jr.
Nancy Butler	June Stetson
Barbara Chase	Marian Stetson
Catherine Comerford	Merle Stetson
Helen Craven	Edward Stone
Walter Craven	Ernest Stone
Patricia DeArruda	Frances Stone
Robert DeArruda	Raymond Stone
Alice Dowling	Richard Stone
William Dowling	Beatrice Strickland
Bertha Duehring	George Strickland
Nancy Ewald	Georgia Strickland
Roger Ewald	Ronald Strickland
Betty Ford	Sandra Strickland
Helen Hathaway	Sarah Strickland
John Hathaway	Dale Swift
Lena Henshaw	Lawrence B. Swift
Luther B. Hoard	Warren Sylvester
Mabel Hoard	Nancy Tibbets
Elizabeth Howes	Andrea Travers
Harriet Hunter	George Travers
Robert Hunter	Gregg Travers
Beatrice Jack	Iona Travers
Amelia Johnson	Clarence Trenouth
Mildred Lang	Frances Trenouth

Ruby Linn
David Mackie
James Mackie
William Mackie
Carl Maronn
Jeffrey Maronn
Larry Mattos
Betsy Perry
Elwell Perry
Jeane Perry

Roscoe Trenouth
John Turner
Sharon Turner
Wilfred Turner
Mabel Vincent
A. Marshall Walker
Forrest Washburn
Vivian Washburn
Lena Winslow

MEMBERSHIP 1984

Eleanor Adams
Ronald Adams
Vernon Adams
Lee Albrecht
Rebecca Albrecht
Edith Ames
Vera Ashley
Ethel Bindon
Erland Brailey
Robert Campbell
Keith Champoux
Catherine Comerford
June Comerford
Dolores Dean
Eric Dean
James DeArruda
Patricia DeArruda
Robert DeArruda
Denise DeYoung
Bertha Duehring
Beverly Griffith
Stanley Griffith
Chris Gupton
Fred Gupton
Linda Juranty
Paul Juranty
Amelia Johnson
Christopher Kelley

Mindy Maronn
Betina Norman
Bruce Norman
Melissa Norman
June Paduch
Elaine Pasteris
Andrea Perry
Brian Perry
Bernice Pierce
Eva Reed
Faith Reed
Laurel Rego
Catherine Russo
Donna Russo
Joseph Russo
Madelyn Scott
Carolyn Sedgley
John Sedgley
Danielle Slight
Janice Souza
Althea Stetson
Douglas Stetson
Marian Stetson
Merle Stetson
Jacque Stone
Beatrice Strickland
George Strickland
Ronald Strickland

Sandra Kelley   Sarah Strickland
Stanley Kelley   Gail Terry
Mildred Lang   Clarence Trenouth
Richard LeBeau   Roscoe Trenouth
Joyce LeClair   Mabel Vincent
Suzanne LePage   Elsie Wheeler
Ruby Linn

NEW MEMBERS 1985

Barbara S. Chace   Mark Geisser
R. Jonathan Chace   Nancy Hambly
Andy Dunham   Barbara O'Shea
Karl Eklund   Mary Parent
Sally Snow-Eklund   Stanley Pasteris
                             Jarred Slight

ASSOCIATE MEMBER
Louise Brady

Chapter 8

MINISTERS

Year	Minister	Note
1853	Moses Brown	
1869-71	Hiram Sweet	
1871-74	John G. Gammons	
	George Macomber	
	Mr. Touser	
	Mr. Worthing	
	Mr. Brown	
1874-75	Solomon P. Snow	
1875-78	James B. Washburn	
1878-79	Francis D. Sargent	
1879-80	Charles H. Farnsworth	
1880	Charles Stokes	
1881-83	Charles T. Hatch	
1883-84	George Hudson	
1884-86	J. O. Denning	
1886-87	John Livesay	
1887	J. A. Morrison	(1 month)
1887-90	George H. Flynn	
1890	Benjamin C. Gillis	(1 month)
1890-92	Benjamin J. Chew	
1892-93	Francis B. White	
1893-95	C. E. De La Mater	
1895-96	H. H. Critchlow	
1896-98	E. B. Gurney	
1898-02	Charles S. Thurber	
1902-05	Ernest W. Belcher	
1905-07	Thomas A. Hodgdon	
1907-08	E. H. Tunnecliffe	
1908-11	Joseph Hollingshead	
1911-14	Curtis W. Chenoweth	
1914-16	Alfred E. Kent	
1916-18	Philip A. Ahern	
1918	Donald Dorchester	(Apr-Sept)
1918-19	Howard B. Lewis	(Sept-Apr)
1919-20	Ernest McP. Ames	
1921-23	S. M. Harris	
1923-25	Frank Chamberlain	

1925-26	Manfred A. Carter
1926-29	George Smith Brown
1929-36	Clinton E. Bromley
1936	Arthur Wadsworth (2 months)
1936-37	Howard Busching
1937-38	Zerna V. Arthur
1938	Clayton Small
1938-41	Richard Chrystie
1941-44	Joseph W. Eller
1944-51	Joseph H. Pritchard
1951-52	William C. Moore
1952-56	S. Howard Davidson
1956-59	John Cermak
1959-61	James Prickett
1961-62	Robert A. Rowe
1962-64	Harold French
1964-67	J. Michael Miller
1967	George E. Jaques (interim)
1967	R. Kenneth Manning Jr.
1968-72	Richard Karpal
1973-75	Richard Dean
1976-83	Paul Whitteberry
1983-86	Alan Ben Levy Previto
1987-90	Susan B. Carlson
1990-	Beverly E. Stenmark

The Myricks Methodist Church has mostly been supplied with student ministers. They generally attended theology school while serving in Myricks.

Moses Brown seems to have been very dedicated to the Myricks Church. He was instrumental in the funding of the new church building in 1853.

Hiram Sweet's appointment is documented in the following letters.

"Rochester March 19th "/69
Dear Brother Hoard: our Conference has

stationed Me at Myricks + I Shall Be
there as I promised you one week from Next
<u>Sabbath</u>. Myrick Delegate was not Present
at our Conference But they thought it
Desirable with your wishes that Such an
appointment would Suit you after I told
them what had Been Don + Br Brown Said
that you were making Calculations for Me.
I Shall Be Ready to Move my Family after I
see you.
The Good Lord Bless Myricks ------

                              Yours Truely
George Hoard Esq   Hiram Sweet
Myricks"

The other side of this letter reads:

"Br Hoard Dear Brother I have Just
Received yours of 17th + I suppose the
within Letter will Meet your approlation.
I Shall Commense Labors on next Sunday
with your People.

                              Yours Truely
Rochester March 22   H Sweet"[1]

<u>The Taunton Directory</u> 1870 - 71 states:

"Protestant Methodist Church. Myrickville
organized about 1850. Pastor, Rev. Hiram
Sweet. Chorister, Seth F. Staples."

John G. Gammons was born January 7,
1836. He joined the ministry in 1873. He
died on January 29, 1912, and he is buried
in Westport Point, Massachusetts.

Solomon P. Snow was born on August 10,
1811. He entered the ministry in 1836,
and he died on December 17, 1886. He is

59

buried in Exeter, New Hampshire.

James B. Washburn was born on October 11, 1819, and he joined the ministry in 1894. He died on September 8, 1905, and he is buried in North Marion, Massachusetts.

Francis D. Sargent was born on March 19, 1840, and he entered the ministry in 1868. He was buried in Ludlow, Vermont after he passed away on March 21, 1916.

Charles Stokes was born on December 21, 1817. He entered the ministry in 1834. He and his wife, Mary, were given a surprise 40th wedding anniversary party while in Myricks, and they received some "handsome" gifts. He died on April 26, 1881, and he was buried in Staples Street Cemetery in East Taunton, Massachusetts. His wife died on April 30, 1882, and she is buried next to her husband.

Charles T. Hatch was born on September 24, 1854. He joined the ministry in 1885. He died on October 26, 1934, and he is buried in Falmouth, Massachusetts.

John Livesay was born on June 24, 1820, and he entered the ministry in 1844. His wife died on September 10, 1886. John passed away on June 17, 1893, and he is buried in Fall River, Massachusetts.

Francis B. White was the first minister who recorded that he was a full time student during the week.

Harold H. Critchlow was born in Butler, Pennsylvania, and his wife Jennie H. was born in Laconia, New Hampshire. After

REV. GEORGE H. FLYNN

REV. C. E. DE LA MATER

serving in Myricks he went on to serve in Acushnet, North Dighton, Fall River, Stoughton, and New Bedford, Massachusetts, as well as towns in Rhode Island and Connecticut.

E. B. Gurney was married and had a daughter named Mildred.

Charles S. Thurber was born in East Bridgewater, Massachusetts on May 22, 1864. He married Minnie I. Pierce who died in 1948. He was a pastor in Stoughton, Chilmark, and East Falmouth, Massachusetts, and Wakefield, Rhode Island. After he left Myricks he was Chaplain at Seamen's Bethel and Mariner's Home in New Bedford, Massachusetts from 1910, until his death at age 91 in August 1955. He planned to attend the 100th anniversary celebration at Myricks. Ethel F. Blaisdell, a niece of his late wife, wrote <u>And God Caught An Eel</u> which included information about Reverend Thurber's ministry in Myricks. The last entry in the Myricks records by Reverend Thurber was:

"The people have been very kind to the pastor and his family, and the prayer of pastor and people is that God will graciously add his blessing upon all our efforts to do good, while we help our fellow man on toward God."

Ernest Belcher was born on November 14, 1870. He entered the ministry in 1892. He was married to Minnie E. and had two sons born while he served in Myricks. Lawrence W. who was born on May 14, 1902, and Kenneth H. who was born on August 17,

1903 and died on November 22, 1904. When he left Myricks the congregation gave him a gold watch. After passing away on March 19, 1920, he was buried in North Abington, Massachusetts.

Thomas A. Hodgdon was born in 1846. He entered the ministry in 1886, and he died on January 27, 1929. He is buried in Malden, Massachusetts.

Joseph Hollingshead was born on February 20, 1839. He entered the ministry in 1859, and he died on April 9, 1919. He is buried in Norwich, Connecticut. Upon leaving Myricks he wrote:

"In this my last report I wish to express my appreciation of the efforts and liberality of the few members and friends of the church. They (illegible), but they have given freely of their substance freely and cheerfully for the support of the Church and the benevolences of the Church. Surely the Lord has blest what they have done for the little Church has enjoyed temporal prosperity. I doubt whether any charge in the Conference has done better taking into account numbers and means. Feb. 1th 1911"

There was no pastor for part of 1911. Reverend Joseph Hollingshead preached one Sunday. Several Sundays Reverend J. Adams, a local preacher from Pawtucket, Rhode Island, spoke.

Reverend Curtis W. Chenoweth of West Virginia was appointed pastor on September 17, 1911. He and his wife, Jessie H. had a daughter on March 18, 1912. They named her Edith.   They had several other children. He wrote in 1912:

"After six months here I am convinced that Myricks is a good field. I see no reason why, the right method extended over a sufficient period, should not add that entire number to our regular Sunday congregation. But whether or not we are able to do all we hope in this direction I am sure that this church has a future.

Our public school is crowded with children. If our Sunday School reaches them now - five years hence they will be church helpers. We have now a band of helpers composed of both young and older people who really put an earnestness into their work that is bound to bring good results.

I wish here to record my gratitude to every member of that company. And at the same time express the conviction that no where in New England or beyond is the Myricks people excelled in doing things. Upon that fact I base the opinion that this church has a prosperous future."

Philip A. Ahern was born in London, England. His wife's name was Hannah Davis, and they had a daughter named Phyllis. His first assignment in the Southeastern Conference was at Myricks. His next parish was at Fall River, Massachusetts.

Ernest McP. Ames was born in Lamikai, Oahu. His children were Merle, Leola, Mrs. Lorraine Morse and Mrs. Christie Marsh. He served for many years, coming

MRS. KENT

Back: Mrs. Blake, Fanny Staples, Mrs.
Haskell, Rev. S. M. Harris, Mrs. Harris.
Middle: Mrs. Lillian Wade, Mame Hoard,
Mabel Turcott. Front: Rhoda Hoard, Addie
Whittaker, Polly Pierce, Hattie Pierce

to Myricks from Freetown and Acushnet, Massachusetts. He lived in Acushnet, and he did not use the parsonage. His next assignment was in New Bedford, Massachusetts. Upon leaving Myricks he wrote:

"It is with regret that there is not more progress in the spiritual life of the church. Still there is much to be grateful for. The people are warm hearted. 'I was a stranger and they took me in' and in no place have I enjoyed pastoral visitation more than on this charge...I have but one desire and that is that the church of Myricks may prosper."

Reverend Manfred A. Carter wrote on the occasion of the 100th anniversary of the church:

"Hampden, Maine

August 6, 1953
Anniversary Committee
Myricks Church

Dear Friends

Best wishes for your anniversary. I regret that I have already agreed to speak on August 16th. This prevents my attendance.

In my brief ministry, 1925 to 26, there were heating and lighting improvements at the church, baseball and soccer teams, and a community youth group that used the church hall, which you have since improved. It was a happy year, with good people, and the memories are pleasant.

REV. MANFRED A. CARTER

Sincerely
Manfred A. Carter"

George Smith Brown was born on April 28, 1895. He was president of the Oregon Anti-Liquor League, Inc. He and his wife, Dorris P., had a son, Jarvis, who became a minister. Reverend George Smith Brown died on October 8, 1961. The Myricks Church received a letter from Reverend Brown on the occasion of the 100th Anniversary of the church which read in part:

"Mrs Brown and I would be very happy to go to renew old acquaintances. Having had more experience now, we would like even to be your church leaders again. The things you folks have suffered from young and green ministers thru the years prove your durability thru thick and thin. Your kindness to your ministers builds them into Christians of faith and more patience than they ever had before."

Clinton E. Bromley was born in Jewett City, Connecticut, son of Charles B. and Frances (Gates) Bromley. He graduated from Drew Theological Seminary in New Jersey. He was married twice. His first wife was Mabel T. Wells, whom he married in 1907. She died in 1918. His second wife was Elizabeth Josephine Winslow who was born in Taunton, Massachusetts. They married in 1921, and she died in 1950. He had two daughters, Winifred Evelyn who lived in Somerville, Massachusetts, and Eleanor Louise (Mrs. Perry E. Ostroff) of Stoughton, Massachusetts, and a son Ernest Raymond of Cincinnati, Ohio, whose wife was Marion. Reverend Bromley served in many locations, including Pennsylvania and

REV. GEORGE SMITH BROWN and DORRIS BROWN

Rhode Island, before coming to Myricks. His last assignment before Myricks was at Pearl Street, Brockton, Massachusetts. After Myricks he went to Westport Point, Massachusetts. He retired, and he lived at 15 Elgin Street in Stoughton, Massachusetts. Reverend Bromley and his daughter Winifred attended the 100th anniversary of the church. He died on January 24, 1965, in his 94th year.

Arthur Wadsworth was born on March 2, 1872, and entered the ministry in 1897. He died on July 31, 1936, just two months after being appointed to the Myricks Church. He is buried in South Dartmouth, Massachusetts.

Howard Bushing wrote in the October 6, 1936, quarterly report:

"I could not in honesty begin my report as pastor in any other way than on the note of appreciation. Mrs. Bushing and I have never been happier in all our lives than we have here in Myricks. We have been here less than two months but nevertheless feel perfectly at home with these folks. They have been friendly as neighbors, generous in their gifts and in their sympathies, loyal to their church, and cooperative to the suggestions that their pastor has had. We could not ask for a better spirit of community interest, and they have added to that a personal graciousness that has literally embarrassed us because sometimes we have not felt altogether worthy of it. ..... a preacher's _first_ church seems to me to be very important for what it may do to his idealism. I want to say, humbly, that I count myself fortunate to have been started in this church."

Zerna V. Arthur wrote on March 6, 1938;

"<u>A Personal Word</u> It is with a feeling of real regret that I come to the last Sunday of my pastorate in Myricks. The people of this church and community have been very kind to Mrs. Arthur and myself, so that it is not easy to move out from pleasant relationships here, no matter how imperative the reasons are. We shall carry with us always the brightest of our stay in your midst, and every moment of memory will be a prayer for your spiritual as well as material prosperity, individually and in every department of the church work."

His next assignment was in Troy, North Carolina.

Clayton Small was born in East Providence, Rhode Island, as was his wife Martha A. W. They had a daughter named Monona W. He served in Rhode Island, Cape Cod, and Southeastern Massachusetts. He was at Marion and Rochester, Massachusetts before coming to Myricks. His next assignment was at Staffordville, Connecticut.

Richard Chrystie was born in Woodstock, New Hampshire. He married Helen H. and had children Richard Holmes Jr. and Barbara May. He served in Hillsgrove and East Braintree before coming to Myricks.

Joseph W. Eller served in Indiana, Oklahoma, Connecticut, and elsewhere in Massachusetts before coming to Myricks.

73

His wife was Agnes Meredith and their children were Meredith Freeman and Gertrude Alice.

Jospeh Henry Pritchard was born on February 20, 1918, in Youngstown, Ohio. He graduated from Fitch High School in Ohio in 1936. He worked for two years as a payroll clerk for Truscon Steel Inc. in Youngstown, Ohio. He attended Texas Christian University in Fort Worth, Texas from 1937 - 40. He married Mary L. Wahl of Fort Worth, Texas on February 12, 1940. His first pastorate was at First Christian Church at DeLeon, Texas from 1940 - 41. He then returned to Youngstown, Ohio as pastor of the Methodist Church at Lowellville, Ohio and worked at Truscon Steel. He received his Bachelor of Arts Degree from Youngstown College in 1944. He and his wife Mary had twin daughters Joanne Marie and Janice Kay who were born in 1941, and two daughters born while he was serving in Myricks, Judith Edna, and Jean Allison. After leaving Myricks, he had a son, Joseph Henry Pritchard Jr., who later became a minister. In 1949, Joseph Sr. attended a summer course at the Institute of Pastoral Care at Worcester, Massachusetts. While serving in Myricks he also preached in Dighton. While in Myricks he attended Boston University School of Theology and received a Bachelor of Sacred Theology in June 1950. He was ordained an elder in the Methodist Church in 1950, at the New England Southern Annual Conference at New London, Connecticut. He served summers on the staff at the Methodist Church camp in Glocester, Rhode Island. Mrs. Pritchard also served at the camp as a girl's councillor. He preached his last sermon in Myricks on June 10, 1951. His was the longest pastorship in the history of the Myricks Church. Upon leaving Myricks he went to the First Methodist Church, Modesto, California. There he served as associate pastor, one of four pastors of the church. His work was primarily on evening programs, youth programs and as a councillor. He also was one of the organizers of the Nevada Council of Churches while pastor at Epworth United Methodist Church of Fallon, Nevada in 1954. For ten years he served on the faculty of the University of Utah School of Alcohol Studies. While in Nevada he served on the Nevada Board of Parole Commissioners from 1961 - 64. In 1964, they were residents of San Leandro, California where he was senior pastor of the First United Methodist Church. In 1967, they visited Myricks. They stayed with Ernest and Frances Stone. An open house was held in their honor at the home of Robert and Patricia DeArruda. Reverend Pritchard was a guest speaker at church that Sunday. In 1970, he became Administrator of the Division of Alcoholism and Drug Abuse for the state of Nevada. In 1973, he assumed the pastorate at the First United Methodist Church of Carson City, Nevada.

William Clifton Moore, the son of a Methodist minister, was born and raised near Memphis, Tennessee. He received his A. B. Degree from Lambeth College, Jackson, Tennessee. He earned his B. D. Degree from the Theological School, Emory University, Atlanta, Georgia. He served five years as a pastor and three as

REV. JOSEPH PRITCHARD and FAMILY

director of youth programs in the Memphis Conference of the Methodist Church. He served one year on the staff of the youth department of the general board of education. He came to Myricks from Nampa, Idaho where he served as executive secretary of the board of education of the Idaho Conference of the Methodist Church. William Clifton Moore served both the Myricks and Dighton parishes. He had a wife, Frances, and two daughters, Marilyn and Anne. He worked toward a Doctor of Philosophy Degree at Boston University while in Myricks. After serving in Myricks he moved to Auburndale, Massachusetts. In 1967, when his wife died, he was a professor at Boston University School of Theology.

Howard Davidson arrived in Myricks on July 1, 1952. He and his wife Maxine had three children. Their names were Edward, Jeannette Lee and William. He served in both Myricks and Dighton. He later served in Bloomfield, Illinois.

John Cermak, the son of a Methodist minister, received an A. B. Degree from Albion College. He and his wife Adele had sons named Douglas and Daniel. They came to Myricks after he served as pastor of the Washington Heights Methodist Church, Battle Creek, Michigan. He was pastor in both Myricks and Dighton. While in Myricks he studied for a Sacred Theology Degree at Boston University School of Theology.

Harold W. French and his wife Rosemary had three children. Their names were Steve, Mark and Becky. He was a patient at

REV. S. HOWARD DAVIDSON
and MAXINE DAVIDSON

Massachusetts Osteopathic Hospital in Jamacia Plain while serving in Myricks. While he was ill Edmund Ogg performed the duties of the minister. Harold received a Master of Sacred Theology Degree from Boston University on June 7, 1964. The congregation held a surprise farewell supper at Grove Hall for Harold and Rosemary before they left on June 8, 1964.

Before leaving he wrote:

"We are indeed grateful for the privilege of having known you and lived in your midst these two years. It seems very short for us, and we are deeply conscious that we leave many tasks uncompleted, many relationships scarcely more than begun. Yet it has been a time rich in meaning for our family. The memory of your warmth, your thoughtfulness, your energetic initiative in getting things done will leave an indelible impression upon us."

His next assignment started on July 1, 1964, at Westmar College in LeMars, Iowa, as college chaplain, where he served for four years. In 1969, he was preaching in seven United Church of Canada Congregations.

John Michael Miller, Jr. attended DePauw University, Greencastle, Indiana for one year. He then attended the U. S. Naval Academy at Annapolis, Maryland for four years, graduating in June 1956, with a Bachelor of Science Degree in Marine Engineering and Electrical Engineering and a commission as an Ensign, USN. He served eight years in the Navy, resigning in Vallejo, California ten days before his

REV. HAROLD FRENCH and FAMILY

arrival in Myricks on June 20, 1964. He married his wife, Dolores Quartz of Alverton, Pennsylvania in 1956, in Long Beach, California. She was active in the community and church. She had been working as a nurse for years, and while in Myricks, she helped care for the sick in the community. She spent a lot of time with Edward Winslow who died on February 1, 1966. She also sang in the choir. They had two daughters, Ruth Ellen and Jeanette. Mike, as he was known, preached in both the Myricks and Dighton Churches, and then after November 30, 1965, in the Myricks Methodist and Berkley Congregational Churches. While serving these churches, he was enrolled in the Boston University School of Theology working for a Bachelor of Sacred Theology Degree (STB). He received magna cum laude honors at the senior honor convocation ceremonies. He preached his last sermon in Myricks on June 25, 1967. J. Michael Miller was ordained a member of the New England Southern Conference of the United Methodist Church and an elder in the church in June 1968.

He joined the staff of Boston University in the fall of 1968, working for the Director of Field Education while pursuing a PhD in Biblical Studies, Old Testament. He was awarded the PhD in June, 1972. He served as Associate Pastor to Reverend Donald H. Freeman, one year, and Reverend Francis C. Wilson, three years, at the Centre Methodist Church, Malden, Massachusetts. From 1971 - 1978 he served at Woodridge United Methodist Church in Woodridge, Illinois. He was Associate Professor of Old Testament at Oral Roberts

REV. J. MICHAEL MILLER and FAMILY

University from 1978 - 85. Reverend and Mrs. Miller returned to Myricks in 1981 to attend the dedication of the carillon in honor and memory of the Trenouth Family. From 1985 - 89 he served at the First United Methodist Church, McHenry, Illinois. His latest transfer was to the Roswell United Methodist Church in Roswell, Georgia as Minister of Education in 1989. That congregation has 7,000 members. Dolores, who continued nursing until 1995, is active in the church, and she enjoys singing in their choir. Ruth Ellen and Jeanette are both married with a total of eight children.

George E. Jaques served as interim pastor in 1967.

Kenneth Manning was married to Barbara Cannell. They had three children, Peter, Stephen, and Kevin. Kenneth served in World War II. He graduated from Northeastern University in 1947. In 1950, he graduated from the Boston University School of Law, and in 1951, he earned a Masters Degree in Law. He was formerly employed by the John Hancock Insurance Co. While in Myricks, he was studying at the Boston University School of Theology. He was pastor at the Berkley Congregational Church at the same time he served Myricks. He resigned to return to the company where he formerly worked. He moved out of the parsonage on July 16, 1968.

Richard S. Karpal arrived in Myricks from Oneonta, New York. He stayed with Walter and Helen Craven until the parsonage was vacated. He had a wife, Martha, and a son, Raymond. His last sermon in Myricks

REV. RICHARD KARPAL and FAMILY

was preached on June 25, 1972. They then went to Rockville, Maryland to the United Methodist Church there. In 1987, he was serving at Emmanuel United Methodist Church in Beltsville, Maryland.

Richard L. Dean was born in Boston, Massachusetts in 1930. He grew up in Worcester and worked for the Worcester Telegram + Gazette. He served in the Navy during the Korean War. He attended Worcester Jr. College and received an AA Degree in 1957. He received an AB in 1959, from American International College. In 1960, he attended the Boston University School of Theology. His first assignment was at Cherry Valley Methodist Church in Leicester, and he has served at the United Church of North Truro, and Westport Point Methodist Church. He has taught at Oxford, Provincetown High School, and Westport High School. He has been an instructor of psychology at Bristol Community College, and Executive Director of the Fall River branch of the NAACP. He also had his own practice in marriage counseling. Reverend Dean and his wife Beverly have a son Thomas. Beverly was a charge nurse at Country Garden Nursing Home in Swansea, Massachusetts. His last Sunday in Myricks was December 26, 1976. He then went to the Provincetown District.

Paul Whitteberry is a native of Indiana. He married Marjorie Knapp of Westchester County, New York. Their children are Susan (Mrs. Guy Freesen), Barbara (Mrs. Todd Zachs) and David. Reverend Whitteberry received a Bachelor of Arts Degree with high honors in 1949, from Olivet Nazarene College. He also earned a

Bachelor of Sacred Theology, Master of Arts in Philosophy, and Master of Sacred Theology Degrees at the Boston School of Theology and Boston University Graduate School. He has served as pastor in Boston, Brighton, Holyoke, Pittsfield, Sommerville, and Natick, Massachusetts and in Connecticut and Ithica, New York. While in Myricks he also served as pastor of the Trinity United Methodist Church in Taunton. Reverend Whitteberry made the following statement:

"The strength of the Myricks Church is not based on its numbers but on the devotion of its members."

April 9, 1977, was Reverend Whitteberry's 25th anniversary as an ordained minister, having been ordained by Bishop John Wesley Lord. On April 9, 1977, during worship services at both churches, Reverend Whitteberry was reconsecrated as ordained elder of the United Methodist Church by Bishop Edward G. Carroll. Bishop Carroll was resident bishop of the Boston area of the United Methodist Church. Bishop Carroll preached that day. This marked the first time a bishop ever preached in Myricks. After serving in Myricks Reverend Whitteberry's next pastorship was at Somerset United Methodist Church. He and his wife owned and operated the Plymouth Rock KOA Kampground of America, Inc. in Middleboro, Massachusetts.

Alan Previto was born in New Orleans, Louisiana. He graduated from Burmingham Southern College. He had his calling in 1965, at a United Methodist Church Rally. He is a musician with four recorded albums. He graduated from Boston University School of Theology in 1983. He began his ministry in Myricks in June 1983. Reverend Previto married Miriam (Mindy) Maronn on July 20, 1985, while he was a minister in Myricks. During his time in Myricks the membership of the church went from 37 to 90. He preached his last sermon in Myricks on December 28, 1986. He was transferred to the First United Methodist Church in Woonsocket, Rhode Island.

Susan Carlson came to Myricks on January 4, 1987, as a full time minister. Susan and Richard Carlson had three daughters, Erika Karin, Kristina Britt, and Svea. She last preached in Myricks on June 17, 1990, after serving here for three and one half years. She was appointed Chaplain at the Health and Retirement Center in East Providence, Rhode Island, and pastoral counselor at the Interfaith Counseling Center, New Bedford, Massachusetts. She later became associate pastor at Trinity in Springfield, Massachusetts. On July 1, 1995, she was appointed to Ashbury United Methodist Church in Warwick, Rhode Island.

Beverly E. Stenmark was ordained as a Deacon on June 20, 1992.

1 Old Colony Historical Society, Taunton, Massachusetts, Folder VM989C.

Chapter 9

WORSHIP SERVICE

In 1878, "The convention of churches was held in the M. E. Church at Myricksville, Wednesday, and the house was filled to its entire capacity."[1] Speakers were Reverend I. C. Thatcher of Lakeville, Reverend B. S. Bachelor of New Bedford, Reverend E. Burroughs of East Freetown, and Reverend Wood of Assonet.

In 1892, approximately ninety parishioners attended the morning services, with an average of about forty in the evening. On September 13, 1893, a weekly collection was instituted during services to help with the current expenses of the church. In 1919, due to an order by the Board of Health, there were no services for four weeks in September because of an epidemic of Influenza.

On May 17, 1965, 100 members of five Masonic Lodges attended church services in Myricks. On St. John's Sunday in 1966, the Masons from the Taunton area again attended church in Myricks.

One very significant part of every worship service is the music. Over the years many talented women have supplied piano and organ music. Among those who have provided these services are:

Elizabeth Batcheldor	Betsy Perry
Barbara Chace	Barbara Sellars
Marianne Dow	Priscilla Spring
Jean Farnam	Patricia Stetson
Rita Harrison	Patricia Stone

Bernice Holmes   Alice R. Waterfield
Dorothy B. Jack
Carolyn Melesky
June Stetson Paduch
Dorothy Stetson Peirce

Reverend Gordon L. Washburn provided violin music on occasion. Reverend Alan Previto played his guitar during some services.

In addition to instrumental music, Myricks has had active choirs. In the 1870's, Seth F. Staples was chorister. In 1903, an entry in church records reads: "A choir now sings" with Miss Lena Farmer as leader. About 1924, Reverend Frank Chamberlain wrote:

"A Choir has been formed with a goodly number of voices also a Violin and Sello which adds much to the services."

In 1929, Warren A. Holmes was choir director. In 1931, Percival Staples was the president of the Young People's Choir, and in 1932, Dorothy Jack was president. A twelve member Girl's Choir sang at services in 1936. Patricia DeArruda was director of a sixteen member choir in 1965. Avis Walker organized and directed a Junior Choir in 1970. Douglas and Dale Stetson were a two member choir for quite a while in the 1970's. In 1990, in addition to singing on Sundays, the choir sang at nursing homes several times.

The first organ at the church was mentioned in the document paying Moses Brown for work on the new church building (Chapter 3). It listed $30 paid for an

MYRICKS

Methodist Episcopal Church

Rev. E. B. Gurney, Pastor.

SUNDAY SCHOOL LESSON

For Next Sunday.

Next Sunday will be the last Sunday of the quarter and the review will take the form of a written examination. The school will be divided into three sections.

Section 1. Classes 1, 2, 3 and 4.

Prizes, Bible, a good book.

Section 2. Classes 5 and 6.

Prizes, a good book, year's subscription to the Classmate.

Section 3. Classes 7 and 8.

Prizes will be given for the best attendance,

SUNDAY, DECEMBER 19, 1897.

HOURS OF SERVICE:

Preaching Service,	11.00 A.M
Sunday School,	12.15 P.M
Epworth League,	6.30 P.M
Gospel Service,	7.00 P.M
Midweek Service (Thursday),	7.30 P.M

The Expense of these Calendars is borne by the Pansy Club.

Order of Service.

Doxology.

Invocation.

Responsive Reading. Ps. 126.

Hymn, No. 19.

Scripture Lesson. Mat. 13 : 24-30, 36-43

Prayer.

Notices and Offertory.

Hymn, No. 575.

Sermon.   Rev. T. J. Everett, Presiding

Elder New Bedford District.

Closing Prayer.

Hymn, No. 811.

Benediction.

Notices and Comments.

The Pansy Club realized about $25 at their recent sale.

Miss Kelley will give her Recital in the Church Monday evening, rain or shine.

The subject this evening will be that announced for last Sunday evening, "Fare, Please."

Santa Claus will hold a reception in the Hall Friday evening and Christmas exercises will be held next Sunday evening.

A business meeting of the League will be held with Edith Haskins Tuesday evening. Every member is urged to be present.

The pastor hopes to be able next Sunday to announce a very helpful series of services with which to commence the new year.

The study of Romans will be taken up at the Thursday evening service this week. These Bible Studies are very interesting and instructive. All are cordially invited.

91

THE MYRICKS CHURCH
(Methodist Episcopal)
Rev. Howard C. Busching, Pastor.

Sunday, Aug. 23, 1936

MORNING SERVICE, 11 A.M.

Call to Worship

Opening Hymn, No. 32

Collect and Lord's Prayer

Choir selection

Psalter, 34th. Sunday

Gloria Patri

Apostle's Creed

Pastoral Prayer

Offertory and response

Notices and Hymn, No. 197

Scripture Lesson

Sermon

Hymn, No. 180

Silence and Benediction

I cannot say, and I will not say
That he is dead, he is just away!
    With a cheery smile
    And a wave of his hand
He has wandered into an
    unknown land.

Think of him faring on, as dear
    In the love of There,
    as the love of Here.
Think of him still as the same,
    I say,
He is not dead — he is just away!

    In loving memory of
        Lawrence Stetson.

COMING EVENTS

Aug. 26 –
    The annual CLAM BAKE, to be
    held at GROVE HALL.
    Sponsored by the COMMUNITY
    CLUB and the WOMEN'S
    FRIENDLY SOCIETY. Complete
    menu. TICKETS available
    from Mrs. Edgar Brailey or
    Mrs. Sellars: adults $1.00,
    children under 12, 50¢.
    Begins at 6 P.M. (next
    Wednesday)

SEPT. 2 –
    LADIES AID ALL DAY MEETING
    and DINNER at the STROBRIDGE
    HOUSE.

SEPT. 13 –
    For children and young people-
    SUNDAY SCHOOL and EPWORTH
    LEAGUE opens again. Let's
    get off to a good start
    this year!

#################

Our church LAWN SOCIAL of
Aug. 6 was eminently successful.
$35.51 was cleared for the
church, and the Ladies Aid
made $16.40 in their fancy
work booth. -- Our church people
are all happy over these
results and appreciate the
cooperation that was shown.

The pastor is now the
MYRICKS correspondent for the
TAUNTON GAZETTE. He will
appreciate receiving news items
on Mondays and Thursdays.

August 23, 1936

THE MYRICKS CHURCH
Howard C. Busching, Pastor
May 30, 1937

CANDLELIGHT MEMORIAL SERVICE

CALL TO WORSHIP BY THE PASTOR
HYMN - 72
RESPONSIVE READING:
We praise thee, O God, and bless thy name
We praise thee, O God, and bless thy name
We praise thee, O God, and bless thy name
We praise thee, O God, and bless thy name
We praise thee, O God, and bless thy name
We praise thee, O God, and bless thy name
We praise thee, O God, and bless thy name
We praise thee, O God, and bless thy name
We beseech thee to hear us, O God.
We beseech thee to hear us, O God.
We beseech thee to hear us, O God.
Thanksgiving, glory, honor, and power
   unto thee, O Lord our God.
All- Glory be to the Father, and to the
   Son, and to the Holy Spirit as it
   was in the beginning, is now, and
   ever shall be, world without end. Amen

THE LORD'S PRAYER
PIANO SOLO - Richard Irving
Offertory
VOCAL SOLO - Iola Busching
Scripture Lesson - Psa. 139:7-14
HYMN - 256
SERMON - The Inescapable God
HYMN - 278
BENEDICTION
   ****

Candles are being burned
tonight in loving memory of:

Mrs. Elsie Demaranville
Mrs. Salome Brailey
Lawrence W. Stetson
Henry H. Horton
Benjamin Anthony
Theodore Anthony
Mr.&Mrs.Willard Rounds
Mrs. W. I. Whitmore
Mr. Frederick Haskins
Mrs. Lavinia Haskins
Mr. William Wilson
Sarah Wright
Minerva Briggs
Elizabeth Hadley
Carrie Rogers
Affie Hervey
Helen Paull
James Paull
Mrs. Chase

There are others also --
friends and relatives ---for
whom candles are burning, but
whose names have not been
printed.
   Let us tonight honor all
the dead by our better living.

   ****

A LAST MESSAGE

   This is the last service that we shall have together
as pastor and people. I want to take just a little space here
to express my sincere feelings about our going away.
   Mrs. Busching joins me in saying that we as a family
have been very happy here in Myricks. You are our first parishioners. We shall never forget you. We shall always cher-
ish the friends that we have made here - some of the best
friends of our lives - and hope that you in turn will not
entirely forget us.
   As your pastor, I wish to say that I am glad to have
had Myricks as my first church. I have been profoundly grateful
to God for his blessings upon our lives together. His spirit of
truth, of love, and of power has been among us, enabling us to
work together for the increase of spiritual values in our church
and community. I believe that we have done much good.
   May you as a church go on to a finer service in the
years ahead. My best wishes attend your new pastor, and I crave
for him your prayers and your faithful support.
   May God also be known to each of you as a personal
Father.

                        Your friend,
                        Howard C. Busching

May 30, 1937

93

organ.   In 1891, an organ was purchased for $100.   In 1907, $60 was raised for an organ.   In 1915, a piano was placed in the church.   The organ was replaced in the 1920's.

In February 1954, the Organ Fund "realized another dream come true" with the purchase of a new organ in memory of loved ones. It was dedicated on November 25, 1956.

A plaque in the back of the church lists:

1954 Donated in Memory of

Charlotte E. Adams
Gerald S. Brailey
Lyle E. Brailey
Silas E. Brailey
Levi P. Churchill
Edmund P. Dean and wife
Louis A. Elliott
Albert F. Haskins Family
Marietta Horton
William Jack Jr.
Mary T. Macomber
Myrick and Farmer Family
Ira L. Rounds, Sr.
Lawrence W. Stetson
Shirley F. Stone
Rev. Charles S. Thurber and wife
Paul S. Trenouth
William Whittemore and wife
Elizabeth M. Williams
Gilbert W. Winslow

On October 3, 1982, an organ was dedicated which was given by LaVon and Ruby Linn and the church family in memory of George Wilson Stetson. The following is part of the speech given at the presentation:

"The gift of the organ is an appropriate memorial to George W. Stetson - he is part of a family of which music played an important part and over thirty years ago he had set aside a sum of money hoping to get an organ for our church. In 1954, it seemed the time had come. With his enthusiasm and the help of his two daughters the necessary money was raised, and an organ was purchased. When he passed away over two years ago money was given to the church in his memory. With that as a nucleus, and a gift from Col. and Mrs. LaVon Linn, his family has been able to buy the new organ."

On December 31, 1995, a new piano was dedicated in the memory of Marian H. Stetson.

The hymnals have often been revised and replaced. New hymnals were bought in 1926. It was voted in 1936, to purchase new hymnals. One new Methodist hymnal has been given each year by the George Stetson family in memory of their son Lawrence W. Stetson. This is done on the Sunday nearest March 2, as Lawrence was born on March 2, 1924. He passed away on August 18, 1936. New hymnals were purchased in 1961. In 1964, twelve hymnals were given by Mr. and Mrs. Calvin Overlock and family in memory of Fred Paull. In 1966, 100 new hymnals were purchased, fifty of these were in memory of loved ones.

In 1967, hymnals were dedicated in memory of Edward W. Winslow, Gilbert Winslow, Mrs. Frank Ames, Helen Marjorie Long Perry, Harvey S. Scott, Mrs. Gladys Staples, Mrs. Lucy M. Staples, Mrs.

Josephine C. Washburn, Mrs. Ethel Greenfield Sellars, William H. Albrecht, Inez M. Mason, Mr. and Mrs. David Mackie, Fred Paull, Levi P. Churchill, Alice E. Churchill, Daniel B. Jones, Charles Whiting, Joseph Mazzola, Edith Chapman, Reverend and Mrs. Charles S. Thurber and friend, Myra D. Anthony, and Mrs. Silas Brailey. In 1991, new hymnals were again purchased.

---

1 <u>Household Gazette</u>, Taunton, Massachusetts, February 21, 1878.

You are invited to attend
a Dedication Service at the
Myricks United Methodist Church
to dedicate a new organ
~ ~ ~ given in memory of ~ ~ ~

George W. Stetson

October 3, 1982 ~ ~ ~ 4 o'clock.
A social hour will follow.
Please reply by Sept. 25, 1982 to
Mrs. George Stetson
4 Mill Street
Assonett, MA 02702

Chapter 10

SUNDAY SCHOOL AND BIBLE SCHOOL

The Sunday School has always been an important part of the church. It has been very well attended through the years. Church records noted that on April 3, 1887, there was no school due to deep snow.

YEAR	SCHOLARS	TEACHERS	AVERAGE ATTENDANCE
1885	55	7	
1886	63	8	
1889	52	8	
1895			42
1908			45
1910			33
1912	48		26
1913	49		
1915	35		
1917	78		
1918	83		
1936	77		49

In the early 1920's, Mrs. C. E. Ashley held a party for the children of the Sunday School as well as the Camp Fire Girls. Candy and fruit were given to those attending. In 1932, a picture was given by Reverend and Mrs Bromley. It was placed in the church for the Sunday School. Col. and Mrs. LaVon Parker Linn had a special interest in the Sunday School and gave coloring books and Christmas Carol books to the school. Recently, Barbara Estes O'Shea, a local artist, gave five paintings to the Sunday School.

On December 19, 1965, Church School Superintendent, Iona Travers, directed a Christmas Pageant. Sandra Strickland portrayed Mary, and Douglas Stetson acted as Joseph. Other cast members were Donna Sedgley, Sharon Turner, Georgia Strickland, Audrey Ashley, June Comerford, Dawn Ashley, Valerie Ashley, William Mackie, Peter Stetson, John Turner, James Mackie, Elwell Perry Jr., Joseph Strickland, Raymond Stone, David Mackie, Robert Smith, Andrea Travers, Gail Stetson, June Stetson, and Lawrence Stone.

Sunday School Superintendents have included Joshua Padelford, P. H. Fletcher, O. H. Atwood, E. P. Dean, Stephen Dow, Mrs. Baker, Crawford Archer, Mrs. George Travers, George Travers, Mrs. Ryan Anderson, Mrs. Silas Edgar Brailey, Mrs. G. Robert Stetson, Mrs. Clinton E. Bromley, William Haskins, Mrs. Merle J. E. Stetson, and Mrs. Gustaf Johnson.

Bible Study groups and Vacation Bible Schools have also been held throughout the years adding to the religious teachings in the community. In 1917, there was a three month Bible Study group. Many times throughout the years there have been adult Bible classes like those held in 1965. In 1985, Bible Study and Sharing Group Meetings were held. That same year, there was a twenty week survey course on the New Testament sponsored by the Trinity and Myricks United Methodist Churches which was presented by Reverend Previto.

In 1928 and 1936, there was a Vacation Bible School held in Myricks. Vacation Bible School was held from August 2 -

August 6 in 1982. About forty four children attended. Vacation Bible School as well as Bible classes were held in August 1990, with the Berkley Congregational Church. Vacation Bible School has been held annually for several years through and including 1995.

SUNDAY SCHOOL PICNIC
Nelson's Grove
About 1894

SUNDAY SCHOOL PICNIC
About 1984

103

Chapter 11

ORGANIZATIONS

LADIES' SEWING CIRCLE

The Ladies' Sewing Circle was formed in November 1871, with thirty one members. The first entry of existing records was dated May 10, 1873. One of the first functions they held was a two day fair and festival on October 29 and 30, 1873. It was held in the Railroad Hall on Grove Street. Sometime between 1908 and 1921, its name was changed to the Ladies' Aid Society. It was later known by the names of Woman's Friendly Society in 1928, United Methodist Women, and in 1941, Woman's Society for Christian Service (WSCS). This organization, under its various names, remained in existence until 1980.

The society held various fund raisers throughout the years to help with church expenses and the needs of the parsonage. In the early 1900's, the members worked on sewing projects, such as quilt making, to earn money. The ladies met once every few weeks, usually at the home of a member, to work on their projects. In the 1920's, they held a Christmas Sale in Taunton. Mrs. Ralph Anthony, on the piano, and Reverend Ernest R. Bromley, on the violin, provided music during a Chicken Pie Supper in the 1930's. Some other events included a Lawn Social which was held on August 6, 1936. At this Social, $81.51 was cleared for the church. The Ladies' Aid made $16.40 in their fancy work booth.

In addition to raising money they sent
cards to residents of the community for
illnesses, births, deaths, weddings,
anniversaries, graduations, Christmas, and
Easter. In 1946, their minutes indicate
they started their meeting with prayer.
They purchased flowers for the church and
for sick members. They worked on tying a
quilt, made holders and cut out aprons for
their May Sale. The sale was held at the
school house, and they netted $32. In
1953, they held a strawberry supper and a
braised beef supper. In 1964, they held
the Annual Strawberry Festival on June
24th. The meal included ham and a salad.
In 1966, there were eighteen members of
the WSCS.

The Society took charge of keeping the
parsonage in repair. They also sometimes
paid the moving expenses of the pastor.

Social activities were also a part of the
organization's functions. In September
1926, sixty members and friends held a
community party at the cottage of Mr. and
Mrs. David Hoard at Crescent Beach,
Mattapoisett, Massachusetts. Other activities the society participated in included
members of the Society attending a weekend
seminar at Camp Aldersgate in Scituate,
Rhode Island in 1953. A one day session
was attended at the Camp in 1966. A
Mother and Daughter Banquet was held on
May 9, 1962. Mrs. Silas E. Brailey was
honored as the oldest person in attendance
while her guest, her great-granddaughter,
Gail E. Stetson, was honored as the
youngest person attending the banquet.

Presidents of the women's group have

The Ladies' Aid Society.

We are the members of the Ladies' Aid Society,
Ev'ry thing we do is done with a nicety;
With willing hearts and helping hands, we're workers don't you see?
How could the church go on without the Ladies' Aid Society.

Who are the members of the Ladies' Aid Society?
None but those but want to be a little busy bee;
We bought the carpet for the church and our own hands tacked it down,
The Ladies' Aid is up to date, they always do things up brown.

We are noted for our suppers, they suit all to a T,
That's how we raise the money to help our treasury;
For all of us are such good cooks, we are experts in that line
And they say our pies are lovely, and the cooks are just as fine.

We are the members of the Ladies' Aid Society,
Every thing we do is done with propriety.
Some wale said that we are talk-y talk-y talk-y
And when it comes to work, that we are lazy, lazy, lazy;
Who ever heard of such a thing, its awful don't you see,
To say such things about the Ladies' Aid Society.

Mrs David Board

LADIES' AID SOCIETY OUTING
DEAN'S COTTAGE - DIGHTON ROCK PARK
1920'S

included Mrs. Angie Wade in 1906, Mrs. Ada Dean and Mrs. Fred Alley in 1929, Mrs. Lena Henshaw in 1935, Mrs. Silas Edgar Brailey in 1936, Mrs. Forrest Washburn in 1938, Miss Hattie Pierce, Miss Polly H. Pierce, Mrs. Edmund P. Dean, Mrs. Clarence Trenouth, Mrs. Bromley, Mrs. Althea Stetson in 1965, and Mrs. Marian Stetson in 1974.

ADULT FELLOWSHIP

Reverend Joseph Pritchard organized the Adult Fellowship in 1947, with about sixteen couples attending. They met once a month, except in the summer months, usually at the home of a member. They held suppers and had social functions. They made contributions to the church and the building fund for the new Grove Hall. In 1953, the Adult Fellowship voted to pay one half of the bill for the installation of a gas stove in the kitchen. They also planned the painting of the church hall in 1953.

OLD GLORY CLUB

In 1919, this club existed, but no facts are known.

EPWORTH LEAGUE

The Epworth League was a forerunner of the Methodist Youth Fellowship. Its objective was to help young people grow spiritually and to have mercy to help others. It was organized in April 1894. Miss Paull was the first president, and there were twelve members. In 1895, Charles Staples was the president of the Epworth League. There were seventeen members and six associates. In 1903, Mrs. A. A. Dean was president. In 1904, Mrs. Ada Dean was the president, Mrs. Helen Washburn, Secretary, and Charles O. Farmer, Treasurer. During this year they raised $98.80 with $75.50 going towards the pastor's salary. In 1906, there were thirty one members with Lena Farmer as president. Miss Mary Whitmore was First Vice President, Clarence Washburn was Second Vice President, Miss DeMoranville was Third Vice President, Miss Ethel Whitmore was the Secretary, and Charles Farmer was the Treasurer. In 1911, there were thirty five members. The Epworth League had twenty four active members in 1919.

The Epworth League was organized again on September 3, 1936, at the parsonage. Meetings were held at 6 P.M. on Sundays with Mrs. Bushing as sponsor. Eleanor Jones was the president. Bettie Joyce Baker, Mildred Jack, Cynthia Pierce, G. Robert Stetson, Frances Ames, Florence Washburn and Mildred Ames were the other officers. At this time the group helped sell subscriptions for the new hymnals for the church. They also presented some plays. In 1938, G. Robert Stetson was the president.

EPWORTH JUNIOR LEAGUE

The Epworth Junior League was formed in July 1895. It was reformed in 1915, and they raised $50 early in the year which was mostly used for the pastor's salary. The Epworth Junior League was reorganized in 1936. Rossa Jones was the president.

PANSY CLUB

In 1897, the Pansy Club was active in raising monies for the church.

UP AND DOING SOCIETY

This society was organized in conjunction with the Epworth League. Their objective was to raise money towards the payment of the pastor's salary.

METHODIST YOUTH FELLOWSHIP (MYF)

The MYF was an organization of young people in the church. In the 1940's, the MYF participated in the church program one Sunday. Patricia Stetson and Alice Young sang a duet, Lucille Valli read a Scripture, Cassie Sellars and Barbara Valli received the offering, and Virginia Anthony gave a prayer.

In 1944, Betty Sellars was the President of the MYF. Merle Stetson was Vice President, and Althea Maker was Secretary/Treasurer. A Halloween Party was held in 1944, with Virginia Anthony in charge of games, Merle Stetson in charge of refreshments, and Rita Garrity and Catherine Sellars in charge of decorations.

Dorothy Stetson was the President of the MYF in 1947. Catherine Sellars was the Vice President, Rita Garrity was the Secretary/Treasurer, Betty Sellars was the Chairman of Worship, Edith Bindon was the Chairman of the Social Committee, and Edith Ames was the Chairman of the Program Committee.

On March 19, 1947, a movie was shown. Admission was twenty cents for children and forty cents for adults. Reverend Pritchard was in charge of getting the tickets. Betty Sellars was in charge of selling the tickets. Stuart Hunter, Robert Hunter, and James Garrity were ushers. Paul Trenouth and James Bindon were ticket collectors. The profit for the show was $14.10.

In 1961, Cynthia Hunter was President of the MYF. Mr. and Mrs. George Travers were sponsors of the MYF for many years. In April 1964, sixteen young people, with Mr. and Mrs. George Travers and Mr. and Mrs. Clarence Trenouth, attended the New York World's Fair. The three day trip, Friday, Saturday and Sunday, included side trips to the Empire State Building and the United Nations. The group stayed at the Commodore Hotel. The MYF started a Lending Library, and in 1965, Donna Sedgley was the librarian. The MYF put on a play "Comin' Round the Mountain" on April 22 and 23, 1966. In 1966, they took a Mystery Ride which ended at Plymouth Plantation. Mr. and Mrs. George Travers and Mr. and Mrs. Merle Stetson accompanied fourteen members on this trip. In May 1966, the MYF journeyed to the Cathedral in the Pines for a Youth Rally.

The MYF supported the church in many ways including financially. They held many fund raisers including scrap paper drives, ham and bean suppers, Swiss steak suppers, strawberry shortcake suppers, chicken pie suppers, and chicken Bar-B-Ques in order to provide this support. On Christmas Eve, they went carolling several years at which time they also delivered baskets to shut-ins. The MYF sponsored a Halloween Party several years. In 1965, they purchased two new tables for Grove Hall. In February 1966, they purchased a new Communion Table for the sanctuary. They helped with roof repairs and improvements to the stairs in front of the church. In 1967, they planted shrubs.

In 1964, Gregg Travers was president of the MYF. In 1964, the officers elected for the coming year were Andrea Travers - President, June Stetson - Vice President, Betsy Maronn - Secretary, and David Stetson - Treasurer. In 1965, the officers elected were June Stetson - President, Gail Stetson - Vice President, Sharon Turner - Secretary, and Raymond Stone - Treasurer. In 1966, officers elected included Donna Sedgley - President, Sharon Turner - Vice President, Sandra Strickland - Secretary, and June Stetson - Treasurer.

PAIRS AND SPARES

The Pairs and Spares group had their first meeting on February 5, 1966. It was a social group organized by Ronald Erickson. They held regular monthly meetings. They held social outings such as bowling. They also held card parties.

MEN'S CLUB/GROUP

In 1927 and 1928, a Men's Club existed. At one point they gave the church $24.90. On March 10, 1985, a Men's Group was formed. They held a Ham and Bean Supper on March 16, 1985. They made monthly visits to the Massachusetts Correctional Institute in Norfolk.

CROSS ROADS CLUB

This was a group of young people who met twice a month at the parsonage. There were eighteen people in attendance at the first meeting. Margaret Dow was President, Irene Melesky was Secretary, and Concord Haskins was Treasurer.

Chapter 12

CLAM BAKES

The Myricks Church held clambakes from September 5, 1882 through 1929, with the 47th and last one being held on August 28, 1929. The first clambake was held at the Rail Road Hall on Grove Street and served 100. Mr. Charles Wade went to Taunton the morning of the first bake with his horse and wagon. He purchased ten bushels of clams for this bake. In 1890, tickets were fifty cents for adults and twenty-five cents for children.

Clambakes were held at the Rail Road Hall for ten years until the church built their own hall. The bakes were then held in the beautiful pine grove at the church. Cedar posts were driven into the ground and then planks and table tops were placed on these to provide seating for 1,000 people. The clambake was held on the last Wednesday of August each year. The clambakes served 1,000 guests and 100 workers. The bakes were a three day affair. The first day was used to prepare for the meal. The second day was spent serving the meal, and the third day was used for cleaning up. On the third day clam chowder, watermelon, and homemade ice cream were served to the help.

In 1897, it was written:

"The Methodist Episcopal church clambake is this week, Wednesday, 25th. The only fault with this bake is it don't come but once a year."[1]

In 1898, Nye's orchestra played at the bake. This bake resulted in the largest attendance to date.

In 1901, the bake took in $222.21. After $180.73 was spent on salaries the remaining $42.48 was deposited in the bank to use towards the pastor's salary. In 1902, of the $229.80 balance after the bake $144.80 was used for the pastor's salary and $85 for painting the outside of the church. In 1903, $175.50 profit from the bake went to the pastor's salary. In 1904, $245.18 was made at the bake. Of this amount, a total of $213.78 went to the pastor's salary, and the balance went to repairing damage from a September gale. In 1905, $224.69 was made with profits going toward the pastor's salary and insurance with the remainder going into the bank. In 1906, $305 was cleared. In 1907, $244.12 was made.

On August 26, 1908, the day of the bake, it was cold and rainy and the bake had to be postponed until the next day. The following is written in church records:

"In August the church met with quite a disaster. For 28 years it has had an Annual Clambake and this has become famous. Great preparations were made to feed the crowd expected which had been increasing every year. Members and friends had worked hard and in utmost harmony. But on the day appointed we had the worst storm of the season and all calculations were spoiled. The next day was threatening with dashes of rain, but it was held and the best was done that could be done under the circumstances."

CLAMBAKE ABOUT 1910

The bake had been planned for 1,000 and only 380 tickets were sold. Only $43.61 was made.

In 1909, there was a very large crowd and many had to be turned away. A total of $301.23 was made. Remarks in the records suggested that the grounds be extended towards the church to make room for the fruit and peanut stands which were too close to the orchestra. They also wanted one or two uniformed officers to be present in the food area in the future. They also felt more attention should be paid to the post card table. They also noted that the dolls were a little too expensive.

On Wednesday, August 31, 1910, the price for an adult ticket was 60 cents. Music was provided by Cole's Orchestra. A total of $296.30 was cleared. In 1911, because of bad weather, $53 was lost. In 1912, it was a cold day, however, "$353.72 plus 38 cents" was made which went to the pastor's salary and for reshingling. Again in 1913, the weather was not favorable with a heavy tempest at one o'clock. A profit of $160.50 was realized. In 1914, the weather was favorable and $304.24 was earned. In 1915, the bake's profits were $270.40. They had a fair day in 1916, and a good crowd brought in $387.07 profit. In 1917, proceeds were $332.08.

The entry in the Clam Bake book for 1918, reads:

"1918 On account of conditions caused by World War - Allied Nations and Germany no bake held this year. Prices for food very high wheat and sugar scarce."

In 1919, $553.95 was earned with 1,000 attending. On August 25, 1920, they made a record $701.90.

In 1921, the tickets were $1.00 for adults and 60 cents for children under 12. Profits totaled $567.67. The following is quoted from the Clam Bake record book:

"1921 We made from our candy table $56.16 I paid Seibel and Baylies $44.05 for candy. Mr Hicks gave some candy. Charles Terry and Dean and Herbert of Assonet gave a box of penny goods each. Mr Collins gave a box of penny goods. Cobb Bates gave five pounds of candy. Mr Elmer Smith gave flower, I think perhaps we may have sold four dollars worth. I think a lot of credit is due to some of the children who helped on my (illegible) around on the grounds with five cents and penny goods. I want to thank the ladies who gave the home made candy for that always sells so well. With best wishes for the coming bakes. Sincerely Alice A. Haskins"

In 1922, due to a severe storm, later believed to be a hurricane, the bake had to be held elsewhere. The record book states:

"Owing to heavy rains we could not hold our bake in its usual place. The place was flooded - water knee deep in places.

Mr. Cornelius Murphy very kindly offered his beautiful grove back of his house and the school house.

119

Everyone put forth their best efforts to make things a success.

The men hustled the dishes from the hall. Tables were put up and everything in readiness within forty-eight hours.

The village and society certainly appreciated what was done to help the reputation of Myricks Clam-bake.

The church is grateful for the community help."

The price of a ticket was $1.25, and profits were $535.24.

Along with the other things mentioned above, in order to hold the bake, the cedar posts used to support the tables had to be moved to Mr. Murphy's grove. Because of this, the bake was held there for several years.

In 1923, $583.06 was cleared. In 1924, profits were $282.86. The following remark is from the Clam Bake book concerning the 1924 bake:

"Notes
The day before the bake was held there was a very hard storm, wires were down, high tides so much so that the clams for the bake could not be dug. Day of the bake dawned fair and bright, crowd kept coming - but no clams. - at first could not get word around as wires were all down.

Sent for frankforts and rolls and served hot dogs for those who wished to stay to dinner. Sold from side tables and held the regular bake next day."

In 1925, profit from the bake was $356.11. In 1926, money from the clambake fund was used to complete lighting in the hall. In 1927, the profits were $77.30.

The 47th Clam Bake was held on August 28, 1929, with 500 guests attending. People came from New York, Pennsylvania, Connecticut, Boston, New Bedford, Fall River, Taunton and other places. Alfred Dow was the general chairman in charge of the bake. Miriam Ashley and Lena Winslow were in charge of tables, Rhoda Hoard - candy, Mildred Lang and Miss Ruby Winslow - ice cream, Marian Stetson and Earnest Brailey - tonic, Bertha Brailey and Mrs. Harry Inghram - frankforts, Ada Dean, Mabel Turcott, Mrs. Alton Hoard, Fannie Staples and Miss Ruth Dean - aprons and fancy work, Mrs. Rogers - lamp shades, Annie Sellars, Mrs. Haskell, Lillian Wade, Mrs. F. G. Sellars and Misses Dorothy and Mildred Jack - luncheon table, Miss Rita York, Marion Horton, Miss Grace Hoskins, Miss Jeanette Jones, and Margaret Dow - peanuts and popcorn, Mrs. Alice Churchill and Lena Henshaw - cake, and Stephen Dow - parking of cars. At this time the bakes were discontinued because so much new equipment was needed.

A small bake was held in 1935 and 1936, for old times sake.

1 <u>Taunton Evening News</u>, Taunton, Massachusetts, Tuesday August 24, 1897, p. 8.

THE FORTY-THIRD ANNUAL
..CLAM BAKE..
OF THE
MYRICKS M. E. CHURCH
WEDNESDAY, AUGUST 26, 1925
ONE O'CLOCK P. M.

MURPHY'S GROVE
NEAR MYRICKS SCHOOLHOUSE
TICKETS $1.25
CHILDREN (UNDER 12) 75 CTS

Nº 739

CLAMBAKE TICKET

The Forty-Seventh Annual Clambake of the M. E. Church, Myricks

Will be held in Murphy's Grove Near School House, Myricks

Wednesday, Aug. 28

Dinner will be served at 1 o'clock consisting of Clams, Fish, Onions, Sweet Corn, Sweet Potatoes, etc.

ENTERTAINMENT

Ice Cream, Confectionery, Cakes, Pies, Coffee, Tea, Fancy Work, etc. will be on sale

PUBLIC PATRONAGE SOLICITED
The 4 p. m. trains, to and from Taunton and New Bedford, will stop at Myricks. Leave N. B. 11:30 a. m. leave Taunton 11:23 a. m.

TICKETS $1.25
Children under twelve, 75c
No tickets will be held after 12:30 unless paid for. If stormy, next day. Tickets limited to 600. Tickets on sale at Mrs. Sellars' Ice Cream Store, Myricks; Pierce Hardware, Taunton.
Bake made by T. P. Rogers, Taunton

au 24 26 27

from <u>Taunton Daily Gazette</u>,
Taunton, Massachusetts,
August 27, 1929, Vol. 156 No. 49 page 12.

Cartoon in newsletter from
Rev. George Smith Brown
mid 1920's

THE FORTY-FOURTH ANNUAL

CLAMBAKE

of the

M. E. CHURCH
MYRICKS

Will be held in Murphy's Grove
Near School House, Myricks

Wednesday, August 25

Dinner will be served at 1 o'clock, consisting of
Clams, Fish, Sweet Corn, Sweet Potatoes, etc.

Ice Cream, Confectionery, Cakes, Pies, Coffee,
Tea, Fancy Work, etc., will be on sale

PUBLIC PATRONAGE SOLICITED

The 12.30 train out of New Bedford (Daylight Saving) also the
4 p.m. to and from Taunton, will stop at Myricks

TICKETS $1.25   CHILDREN under twelve 75c

No tickets will be held after 12.30 unless paid for

If stormy, next day   Tickets limited to 800

Tickets on sale at Mrs. Sellars' Ice Cream Store, Myricks; Pierce Hardware, Taunton

124

Chapter 13

GIFTS AND MEMORIALS

Many gifts and memorials have been given to the church over the years. About July 1881, Miss Paull presented a clock to the church. In 1891, Enos Pierce left the church four shares of Old Colony Railroad stock. About 1900, the Paull brothers gifted the church with a bell. In 1900, Thomas and James Paull gave a clock to the church. Mr. and Mrs. Levi Churchill gave the church a parcel of land in October 1906. In 1908, the James and Mary Pierce Fund consisted of five shares of N.Y., N.H. & H. railroad stock. This stock was declared worthless in 1947.

William H. Pierce left the Church thirteen shares in the capital stock of the Jackson, Lansing and Saginaw Railroad of Michigan. As a condition he required the church to see to the care of the family plot in the Pierce Burying Ground in Lakeville, Massachusetts. These shares had to be sold in 1916. A total of $1,137.24 was realized from the sale of these stocks.

Henry Shove left $2,000 to the church that was received in 1915. In 1916, the widow of Thomas Shores waived the rights to the pew held in his name and requested that it be called the Shores Memorial Corner. In August 1919, Thomas Paull gave two Victory Bonds, each $100, to the church. The First Christian Church of Assonet gave a chandelier and eight wall lamps to the church in June 1923. In 1932, the Edward H. Allen Fund consisted of $400. In

September 1936, a cross was given by friends in memory of Lawrence Stetson. When William Chester Pierce died on November 13, 1942, the William Chester Pierce Fund consisted of five shares of AT+T left in his will to the church. He also left the church five acres of land opposite the church. The church was required to hold at least one religious service a month in order to keep this land, otherwise it would revert to the heirs of William Chester Pierce.

In 1945, a picture, "Christ Knocking at the Door", was given by Mrs. William Jack in memory of her son, William Jack Jr., who was killed in World War II. A Pulpit Bible was given by a friend in memory of Reverend Clinton E. Bromley's wife, E. Josephine Bromley. An organ fund was set up in memory of loved ones in 1953. Reverend John Cermak gave a candle lighter in 1956. The Couples' Club purchased materials and the women of the church made Senior Choir robes in March 1957. Also in March 1957, Mrs. Helen Craven gave Junior Choir robes. Mrs. George Stetson gave covers for the Choir Books.

In 1962, money from the Daniel B. Jones Fund was used to purchase new carpeting. In 1964, the church received four shares of AT+T from Mrs. Florence Brightman and two shares from Mrs. Edward Winslow. Two shares of AT+T were purchased with money given in memory of Mrs. Florence Brightman. One share of AT+T was purchased with money given by Mrs. Edward Winslow. The Daniel B. Jones Memorial Maintenance Fund was established in 1964. He had bequeathed $1,000 to the church which was invested for future repairs or improvements to the property. Limited use of the funds was enforced to perpetuate the memorial. Two flower tables for the altar were given in memory of William H. Albrecht on October 17, 1965. On December 29, 1965, it was voted to add the name of Thomas Paull to the Memorial List. In 1965, the Shove name was also added to the Memorial List. A cabinet was given by Mr. and Mrs. Elwell Perry for the church records. Mr. Perry also rebound and put together binders of church information. In 1966, Miss Ruby Winslow paid for repairs to the clock. On February 20, 1966, a Communion Table, dedicated to youth past, present and future, was presented by June Stetson, MYF president, to Ernest Stone, Lay Leader, who accepted the table for the church. Also, in February 1966, the church received $15,000 from the Estate of Mr. Edward Winslow.

In 1967, Ruby Winslow purchased siding and insulation in memory of her father Mr. Edward Winslow. On April 11, 1967, a repository for the Memorial Book was ordered in memory of Mrs. Bion Pierce. A plaque was affixed to it indicating the memorial. At the same time it was decided to combine the various memorial funds into a single trust fund to be called THE MEMORIAL TRUST FUND. This fund was to carry the following names:

William H. Pierce, James and Mary Pierce, Thomas Paull, Henry Shove, Edward H. Allen, William Chester Pierce, Daniel B. Jones, Edith M. Chapman, and Edward W. and Lena B. Winslow.

Bion L. Pierce, upon the death of his wife Phebe Churchill Pierce in 1967, gifted the church 35.3 acres of woodland on Church Street. This land was sold after 1980, to Elliot E. Cornell. Edith Chapman left the Church $2,000.

Two flower urns were given in memory of Carrie Albrecht in 1968. A Carillon was dedicated on October 25, 1981 in honor of Clarence C. (6-6-1900 -), and in memory of Frances (11-25-1904 - 3-17-1980) and Paul (10-25-1931 - 6-14-1948) Trenouth. Attending this dedication were former Myricks ministers Richard Karpal of Beltsville, Maryland, J. Michael Miller of Tulsa, Oklahoma, and Joseph Pritchard of Carson City, Nevada. The current pastor, Paul Whitteberry, and over two hundred parishioners and friends also were in attendance. The pastor lead the dedication ceremony. A tribute was given by Mrs. Ruby Winslow Linn, and her husband, Col. LaVon Linn, presented a sermon entitled "A Hole in His Shoe." Handbell ringers, from the Norton United Methodist Church, played during the service.

On the same day, a van donated by Ruby Winslow Linn was also dedicated. It was a 1980 Dodge Supervan which could seat fifteen. This van was used to transport children to and from Sunday School, and it was also used as transportation for adults and children attending church services. Catherine Comerford provided most of the driving services for the van. The Council on Aging also had use of the van. When its use declined and it became expensive to operate, it was sold.

On October 3, 1982, an organ was dedicated to the memory of George W. Stetson. The organ was purchased with funds from the Stetson family, memorial funds and funds from Col. and Mrs. LaVon Linn. In 1982, a clock was purchased as a memorial to Bion L. Pierce. Also in 1982, a remembrance fund was established for Lynwood B. Scott. In 1983, memorial funds for Lynwood Scott were used for the lettering on the front of the church. In 1984, memorial funds from relatives, friends and the WSCS were used to purchase draperies in memory of Mrs. Harriet Hunter.

In 1985, Patricia DeArruda purchased a brass cross in memory of George W. Stetson and Lawrence W. Stetson. In 1987, a handicap ramp was built in memory of Carolyn Sedgley. Also in 1987, two ceiling fans were purchased by Mr. and Mrs. Calvin Overlock, and two ceiling fans were given by Julia Currie, Bernice Pierce and Bertha Duehring in memory of their parents. In 1988, a Maundy Thursday Tenebre was given by Mrs. Madelyn Scott in memory of her husband Mr. Lynwood Scott.

In 1989, memorial funds were used to purchase a Baptismal Font in memory of Mrs. Mildred Lang. On Thanksgiving Sunday in 1989, Meredith Ann Stetson, daughter of Merle Douglas and Dale Stetson, was baptized. Her grandparents, Merle J. E. and Althea L. Stetson gave the cover to the Baptismal Bowl in her honor. Memorial funds were used to purchase a communion set in memory of Mr. Frank Ames. Materials for a copier were given by Danielle Slight in memory of her father

Armand Desautels. In 1991, the Memorial Fund for Matthew Lamond was used for nursery furniture, and the Bernice Pierce Memorial Fund was used to purchase New United Methodist Hymnals. On February 27, 1994, a donation was given by Olive Lamond in memory of her loving husband Robert A. Lamond. On December 31, 1995, a memorial service was held for Marian Stetson, and a piano was dedicated in her memory.

Additional gifts have been given to the church including Mr. and Mrs. George Stetson giving an electric pump, and Mr. and Mrs. G. Robert Stetson giving cement blocks for the barbecue pit. A picture was given by Phebe Churchill Pierce. Brass candlesticks were given anonymously. Improvements were made to the parking lot by Mr. Calvin Overlock in honor of his mother Mrs. Francis Murphy. Memorials have also been given in the names of Lamond and W. Knorr.

Chapter 14

OFFICERS AND COMMITTEES

Throughout the years there have been numerous officers on the various committees. The following list is a sample of those who have served their church.

TRUSTEES

1874 George S. Hoard, John Seekell, Charles Farmer, John Allen, William Pierce, James Dean, Joshua Padelford

1878 George S. Hoard, Amos Wade, Joshua Padelford, William Pierce, James Dean

1886 William H. Pierce, James I. Dean, Willard Rounds, Charles Farmer, James Peirce, E. G. Staples

1893 Otis Atwood, W. H. Pierce, E. G. Staples, Otis Farmer

1897 John F. Allen, Ebenezer Macomber, Charles Staples, James Paull, Mrs. Hannah Williams, Mrs. Hannah Cole

1921 Alton Hoard, E. P. Dean, W. F. Haskins, F. DeMoranville, Charles Wordell, Freeman Sellars 2nd, Mrs. Marietta Horton, Mrs. Amy Anthony, Mrs. Ada Dean

1927-28 Alfred Dow, W. F. Haskins, Stephen Dow, Edgar C. Reynolds, Freeman Sellars

1936 Edgar C. Reynolds, S. Edgar Brailey, Forrest E. Washburn, Mrs. Bion L. Pierce, Percival F. Staples, Mrs. Lena Henshaw

1951 George W. Stetson, Daniel B. Jones, Lena F. Henshaw, Phebe C. Pierce, Elsie B. Brailey, Clarence C. Trenouth

1966 Elwell Perry, Ernest Stone, Mrs. Clarence Trenouth, Mrs. Merle Stetson
1974 Frances Trenouth, Althea Stetson, Harriet Hunter, Charles Williams, Jeane Perry, Stephen MacGregor, Elton Rounds, Madelyn Scott, Bernice Pierce

LAY LEADERS/ALTERNATES

1884 Fanny P. Peirce
1892 William H. Pierce/Benjamin J. Chew
1896 O. M. Farmer
1912 Mrs. Anthony/Mrs. C. Washburn
1914 Mrs. Annie Sellars/ Mrs. Dean
1929 Mrs. Brown/Warren A. Holmes
1931 and 1933 Mrs. S. E. Brailey/Lena Henshaw
1934 Mrs. S. E. Brailey/ Mrs. C. E. Bromley
1937 Mrs. S. E. Brailey/ Percival Staples
1960-61 George R. Stetson
1970 Althea Stetson
1974 Althea Stetson/Merle Stetson
1975, 1978, 1982-83, 1988 Bernice Pierce
1990 Bruce A. Lamond
1991 Donna Russo

TREASURER

1875 William Pierce

COMMITTEES

1966 Mrs. Amelia Johnson and Mr. Clarence Trenouth - Wills and Legacies
Mr. Marshall Walker and Mr. Strickland - Insurance
Mr. Walker, Mr. Ernest Stone and Mrs. Strickland - Building Maintenance and Improvement
Mr. Stone - Parsonage

In 1970, the following members were made Honorary Life Members of the Administrative Board:

Frank Ames   William Dowling   Lena Henshaw
Lena Winslow

On February 13, 1972, George W. Stetson was given Honorary Life Membership on the Administrative Board.

In 1978, Honorary members of the Administrative Board were:

Frank Ames   Lynwood Scott
William Dowling   George Stetson
Mildred Lang   Lawrence Swift
LaVon Linn   Clarence Trenouth
Ruby Linn   Mabel Vincent
Bion Pierce

MYRICKS

Methodist Episcopal Church

Rev. E. B. Gurney, Pastor.

OFFICERS

AND

COMMITTEES.

..1897--8..

OFFICERS & COMMITTEES.

Conference Year, 1897—8.

TRUSTEES.—John F. Allen, Ebenezer Macomber, Charles Staples, James Paull, Hannah Williams, Hannah Cole.

STEWARDS.—John F. Allen, O. M. Farmer, Charles Staples, Fannie Peirce, Melissa Farmer, Hannah Williams, Amy Anthony, Mary Allen, Mary Peirce, Amy Staples, Elizabeth Cushing.

MISSIONS.—Fannie Peirce, Hattie Peirce, Mary Peirce, Hannah Cole.

CHURCH EXTENSION.—Hannah Williams, Melissa Farmer, Amy Staples, Mary Allen.

SUNDAY SCHOOL.—Amy Anthony, Fannie Peirce, John F. Allen, Charles Staples.

TRACTS.—Charles Farmer, A. F. Haskins.

TEMPERANCE. — Hannah Cole, Hattie Peirce, Mary Allen.

EDUCATION.—O. M. Farmer, Ada Anthony, Lucy Staples, Alice Haskins.

FREEDMAN'S AID.—James Paull, Amy Anthony, Elizabeth Cushing.

CHURCH RECORDS.—Fannie Peirce.

PARSONAGE AND FURNITURE. — Officers of the Ladies' Circle and Mary Peirce.

MUSIC.—Ada Anthony, Melissa Farmer, Hannah Williams, Elizabeth Cushing.

ESTIMATING PASTOR'S SALARY.—O. M. Farmer, Hannah Williams, Mary Allen, Mary Peirce.

Chapter 15

MISCELLANEOUS

DIRECTORIES

In 1935 and 1936, the Church published "The Myricks Church (Methodist Episcopal) Historical Sketch and Year Book." These Easter Yearbooks were done by the pastor who was assisted by Mrs. David S. Hoard and Mrs. Hannah Williams, and through the cooperation of M. T. F. Littlewood of North Dartmouth, Massachusetts. In addition to advertising, these yearbooks included a message from Reverend Clinton E. Bromley, a brief history of the church, and lists of Church officers, committee members, Society members of Ladies Aid and Women's Friendly Society, Myricks Church School, Church School teachers, and Myricks Epworth League.

In 1968, "Here's Your Church Directory" was written. It included a calendar of events, officers, members and friends of the Myricks and Berkley Churches.

A "Directory of Myricks United Methodist Church" was made in 1983, by Olan Mills. It included pictures of members and their addresses, pictures of the church and Sunday School, a brief history, and a list of pastors.

FAIRS

The Church has held Fairs and Lawn Parties for many years. Mrs. Brailey, Mrs. Bromley, Mrs. Winslow, and Mrs. Washburn were in charge of the 1934 Lawn Party.

Annie Sellars was Chairman of the fair held on August 12, 1939. Iona Travers was the General Chairman for the fair held on August 28, 1965.

Events included:

Doll Carriage, Tricycle and Bicycle Parades, an Auction, Chicken Bar-B-Que, Booths, Fanciwork, Home Baked Goods, Grill, Homemade Ice Cream, Games and a Dunking Stool.

In 1966, Jeane Perry was the General Chairman of the fair.

In the 1990's, the Church began holding a Fall Frolic and Craft Fair. Jacque Stone, who is in charge of the crafts, has been instrumental in the success of this event. They raised $1,000 at the fair in 1991.

MISCELLANEOUS

On October 25, 1904, a fire caused by a locomotive destroyed several buildings in Myricks. The Academy building was among those that burned. The church stored dishes and tables in the Academy and these were also ruined. An inventory of these items was presented to the railroad listing their value at $178.87. The railroad reimbursed the church $125 for their loss.

In 1936, a 200 volume library opened at the church. It was open two hours a day on two days a week.

On June 23, 1962, fifty five members attended a picnic at Charge Pond. In

1984, an All Church Picnic was held at Watson's Pond.

On September 26, 1976, in honor of Berkley's 250th anniversary, an "Old Time Fair" was held at the Myricks Church. Mrs. George Stetson was chairman of this fair. In charge of events were Mrs. Milton Babbitt, Mrs. Clarence Trenouth, Mrs. Roger Chester and Mrs. Eino Silvan. Church services were held at 10 A. M. At 4 P. M. a pet show was held. A Box Social was held at 6 P. M. Events included a hymn sing with Patricia DeArruda as organist and "Tec" White as soloist. Displays included historical items, antiques, plants, flowers, vegetables, old farm machinery, and hand made articles. Other display items were old and new quilts, local materials, blacksmith items, old lamps, local pictures and post cards, old print materials, an old sled, and old tools. At the 250th Anniversary Parade which Berkley held on October 20, the Myricks Church displayed a float paying tribute to John Wesley, the founder of Methodistism in the United States.

In 1984, a Food Pantry was established at the church.

250th ANNIVERSARY FLOAT

Left to Right: Marian Stetson - seated, James DeArruda and Rev. Alan Previto - shaking hands

SOURCE MATERIAL

Records of the Myricks United Methodist Church.

Church articles, materials, and pictures collected by Mrs. Marian H. Stetson now owned by the author.

Newspaper Articles:
  The Republican Standard, New Bedford, Massachusetts.
  Standard Times, New Bedford, Massachusetts.
  Taunton Evening News, Taunton, Massachusetts.
  Taunton Household Gazette, Taunton, Massachusetts.
  Taunton Daily Gazette, Taunton, Massachusetts.
  The Villager, Assonet, Massachusetts.

Old Colony Historical Society, Taunton, Massachusetts, Folder VM989C.

The Ministry of Taunton Vol. 2 (Boston: John Jewett and Company 1853) by Samuel Hopkins Emery.

Souvenir of the New England Southern Conference Vol. 1 (Boston: C. W. Calkins & Co., Printers 1897) by Rev. Kenneth C. Miller.

New England Southern Annual Conference (G. H. Parker, Publisher 1940).

INDEX

This index covers the names of all people mentioned in this book with the exception of the names found on the church membership lists in Chapter 7 and the minister's names at the beginning of Chapter 8.

Bromley, 70 72 99-100 105 109 126 132 135
Brown, 3-5 12-15 23-24 32 58-59 70-71 90
    123 132
Burroughs, 89
Bushing, 72 92-93 110
Campbell, 33
Cannell, 83
Carlson, 43 87
Carroll, 86
Carter, 28 68-70
Cermak, 77 126
Chace, 89
Chamberlain, 90
Chapman, 96 127-128
Chase, 93
Chenoweth, 64
Chester, 137
Chew, 132
Chrystie, 73
Churchill, 20 22 94 96 121 125
Cole, 118 131 134
Collins, 119
Comerford, 29 100 128
Conant, 36
Copeland, 27
Cornell, 128
Craven, 29 83 126
Critchlow, 60
Cudworth, 28
Currie, 129
Cushing, 134
Cushman, 24
Davidson, 77-78
Davis, 3 49 65
Dean, 27 52-53 85 94 100 108-110 119 121
    131-132
DeArruda, 53 75 90 129 137-138
Demaranville, 93
DeMoranville, 110 131
Desaultels, 130
Dow, 27-28 32 89 100 114 121 131

Smith, 100 119
Snow, 59
Spindle, 2
Spring, 89
Staples, 2-3 16 18 51 59 67 90 95 109 121
    131-132 134
Stenmark, 87
Stetson, vii 5 29-30 32-33 36 40 52-53 89-
    90 92-95 97 100 106 109-113 121 126-
    127 129-133 137-138
Stillman, 20
Stokes, 60
Stone, 29 33 75 89 94 100 113 127 132 136
Strickland, 100 113 132
Swartz, 43
Sweet, 58-59
Swift, 2 133
Taylor, 47 49
Terry, 119
Thatcher, 89
Thurber, 43-45 63 94 96
Tibbets, 29
Travers, 29-30 100 112-113 136
Trenouth, 29 33 36 40 83 94 109 112 128
    131-133 137
Trites, 30
Turcott, 67 121
Turner, 100 113
Upham, 3
Valli, 111
Vincent, 133
Wade, 32 35 51 67 109 115 121 131
Wadsworth, 72
Wahl, 74
Walker, 29-30 90 132
Washburn, 24 52 60 90 96 109-110 131-132
    135
Waterfield, 90
Wells, 70
Wesley, 137
Wheaton, 2

White, 43 60 137
Whiting, 96
Whitmore, 93 110
Whittaker, 67
Whitteberry, 85-86 128
Whittemore, 94
Wilbar, 10 12 14 18 20
Williams, 22 94 131-132 134-135
Willis, 16
Wilson, 81 93
Winslow, 52 70 81 94-95 121 126-127 133
      135
Wood, 89
Woodward, 10
Wordell, 131
Wright, 93
York, 32 52 121
Young, 111
Zachs, 85